AN INVITATION TO BE A CONTRIBUTING AUTHOR IN A FUTURE EDITION!

If you would like to be considered for the opportunity of being a contributing author in a future edition of *I Love America*, please let us know!

We have plans for several themed editions of *I Love America*, each featuring 13 contributing authors sharing their stories, ideas, tips, and reader challenges for a stronger America.

Each edition of *I Love America* is "author-funded," meaning a portion of the expense of creating and publishing the book is shared by all the authors.

Fill out the Contributing Author Information Invitation by visiting:

ILoveAmericaBooks.com

I LOVE AMERICA

BOOK 1

MIKE CAPUZZI

AND 13 MILITARY VETERANS SHARING
THEIR IDEAS FOR A STRONG NATION

PUBLISHED BY I LOVE AMERICA BOOKS
A Division of Bite Sized Books

Printed in the United States of America

Print ISBN: 978-1-7341187-4-2
eBook ISBN: 978-1-7341187-5-9

102022

The publisher gratefully acknowledges the contributing authors who granted permission to reprint the cited material.

CONTENTS

PART 1–WELCOME

PART 2–THE 13 VETERANS

PART 3–WHAT NEXT?

"All tyranny needs to gain a foothold is
for the people of good conscience to remain silent."

—Edmund Burke

PART 1

WELCOME

THANK YOU

There are several individuals who deserve acknowledgement and a note of thanks for their support, wisdom, and encouragement. The people below were helpful in bringing this first book to life and sharing it with others.

- ✪ Robert Imbriale
- ✪ Becky Capuzzi
- ✪ Cynthia Thomas
- ✪ Jeff Giagnocavo
- ✪ Eric Bakey
- ✪ Mike Root
- ✪ Keith Lee
- ✪ Bill Harrison
- ✪ Kris Murray
- ✪ Greg Russell
- ✪ Jim Palmer
- ✪ Craig Simpson

- ✪ Lee Milteer
- ✪ Avery Manko
- ✪ Andrew Mazer
- ✪ Aaron Crocker
- ✪ David Frey
- ✪ Denise Griffitts
- ✪ Ron Sheetz
- ✪ Fred White
- ✪ George Burroughs
- ✪ Adam Hommey
- ✪ Julie Boswell
- ✪ Steve Sipress

The 13

I also want to acknowledge and express gratitude for the 13 military veterans who made this book possible. Each of these men and women invested a serious amount of time for this book's effort. Thank you!

Jeff Arnold	U.S. Army
Tracey Brown	U.S. Coast Guard
Gary T. Dyer	U.S. Marines
Jody Gatchell	U.S. Army
Andrew Hibbard	U.S. Air Force
Brandi "BB" King	U.S. Air Force
John Klesaris	U.S. Army
"IRON" Mike Steadman	U.S. Marines
Kevin Stokes	U.S. Army
Jamarrion Tabor	U.S. Navy
Dominic "Slice" Teich	U.S. Air Force
Paul "Roscoe" White	U.S. Air Force
Candace G. White	U.S. Marines

INTRODUCTION

A llow me to share a short story about how the book you are currently reading came about. On June 29, 2022, my friend, Robert Imbriale, made a post on Facebook where he quoted John Stuart Mill who said (in 1867), "*Let not anyone pacify his conscience by the delusion that he can do no harm if he takes no part, and forms no opinion.*" At the end of his post, Robert ended with a single sentence, "*Silence is the wrong answer.*"

These spoke to me because for a long time now, I have been keeping to myself and thinking I could "*do no harm*" by being silent. A day after Robert made the post, I set up a call with him to discuss his post. I wanted to hear more from him. In typical Robert fashion, he inspired me, and he gave some specific ways to think about how I can apply my gifts to make a difference. Little did I know, the seeds he planted on that call would bear fruit just four days later.

July 4, 2022

It was late morning on Independence Day, which I was spending at home with my family. It was a beautiful day as I sat outside further contemplating my conversation with Robert. As I enjoyed the summer weather, I felt a weight to do something that can make a difference for our nation.

And that is when the idea hit me...

My gift is using the written word, in book format, to share helpful ideas and know-how to others. For the past 14 years, I have helped more than 240 business owners, entrepreneurs, and corporate leaders share their important messages by publishing their own books. I also knew that books, pamphlets, and other published content played a huge part in informing and motivating people throughout our history. Remember Ben Franklin's *Poor Richard's Almanack* from history class?

What if I could publish a short, easy-to-read book that featured 13 patriotic Americans who loved America and wanted to encourage others to do their part to keep America strong by writing a single chapter in the book? And just like that the idea for this book came to me.

Then This Happened

As I sat outside, feverishly writing down the ideas that started to flood my brain, a mature bald eagle soared over my house.

I KID YOU NOT!

Bald eagles can be found in the area I live, and I see two or three each year. But seeing one at that exact moment was not a mere coincidence to me. After making sure I wasn't hallucinating, I took this as a divine sign that I had to bring this project to life!

But I wanted to be careful to not add to the noise and negativity that currently surrounds us here in late 2022. We all know the tidal wave of *manufactured* division we are facing in this country. The last thing I want to do is create more negativity because there are no solutions to be found there.

It goes without saying that we have been through a lot, but I know that WE are at our best when WE are united. And as bleak as things appear at times, a study of our nation's history shows us this is not the first time we have been in a rough spot where we have eventually been able to turn things around for the greater good.

So right from the very start, I wanted to make sure this book (and future books in this series) were about giving readers things to think about without telling them what to think.

I Love America Is a Book of Appreciation, Inspiration & Action, Not Politics & Tribalism

My goal with this book is to move past the easy positions of disdain, cynicism, and opposition between left versus right, blue versus red, you versus me and move towards common sense, renewed respect, and sensible action for America. If we can get there, that is the day we change the game.

And what better first step than to feature your fellow citizens? The men and women who have unselfishly served (and for some, continue to serve) their country's military?

I am intentionally giving a voice and platform to everyday Americans. Unless you are a friend or family member, I doubt you will know the folks you are about to meet. And I think that is important. The last thing any of us need is more "advice" from experts, pundits, politicians, talking heads, and activists. I believe the way things get better is if everyday people do positive and meaningful things.

This edition of *I Love America* is about serving those who have served and bringing their stories, ideas and challenges to you. Each chapter contains three distinct sections:

1. The contributing author's profile.
2. Their story, ideas, and insights.
3. Their "reader challenge" (which gives you actionable things to do for America).

It is important for you to know that the 13 veterans you are about to meet are courageous and altruistic men and women who have a profound love for America and have served our country and continue to do so. Their stories are meant to impact you and inspire action. I share this because this is a book by the people, for the people.

Each chapter "sounds" different because it is written by a different person, his or her story in his or her own words. As you read each chapter, I encourage you to focus on the messages shared to see what you can take away from each chapter and use for America's good.

You'll notice a theme weaved throughout this book, which is, *"The American Dream is alive and well, BUT it takes faith, perseverance, and an 'I CAN' attitude combined with ACTION."*

Finally...

I think it is important to share—I am not a veteran. While I came very close to joining the U.S. Navy (in their nuclear engineering program), I decided to remain on the path I was on. In hindsight, I regret not serving my country's military, and if I had to do it all over, I surely would take the different path.

I have a deep respect and admiration for those who choose to serve. I hope this book touches you in some positive way. God bless the contributing authors. God bless you. And God bless America.

—Mike Capuzzi

THIS BOOK SUPPORTS THE TUNNEL TO TOWERS FOUNDATION

The Tunnel to Towers Foundation is non-profit organization whose mission is honor our military and first responders who continue to make the supreme sacrifice for our country. Since its inception, the Foundation has achieved the highest rating from Charity Navigator, the nation's largest evaluator of charities. Ninety-five cents of every dollar donated goes directly to their programs, including:

- The Smart Home Program
- The Fallen First Responder Home Program
- The Gold Star Family Home Program

For every copy of this edition of *I Love America* sold, the publisher will donate $1.00 to the Foundation. For more information about this important organization, visit

https://t2t.org

PART 2

THE 13 VETERANS

Paul "Roscoe" White

Paul "Roscoe" White is a retired 21-year Air Force veteran, with over 1,500 hours as tactical flight instructor, and still teaches and mentors young fighter pilots as a civilian contract F-35 instructor. Paul has also won multiple football championships as a player and as a coach.

He has studied and developed strategies to motivate young men to be better versions of themselves through hard work, good attitudes and solid character traits. Being a flight instructor made him a better coach, and being a coach made him a better instructor.

Always striving for excellence in these two competitive environments made him a better dad and husband. Roscoe believes that anyone can be a champion in life with the right direction and work ethic. To begin your championship run now, visit:

https://1of5Project.com

Chapter 1

EXPLOITING OPPORTUNITY: FROM COTTON FARMER TO FIGHTER PILOT INSTRUCTOR

The promise of opportunity is one of the most fundamental characterizations of the American Dream, and it inspires generations to achieve higher and reach greater potential. My whole life has been a series of events strung together as the result of dumb luck and timing, but sometimes luck plus timing equals opportunity.

I grew up on a cotton farm, and beginning at 10 years old, I was free labor for my dad to grow and gather the crops each year. That experience taught me quite a few lessons, such as how to value money and the value of family, but most importantly, it taught me about working hard to achieve a goal.

I completely failed at my first college attempt, so I enlisted in the Air Force in 1997. My recruiter blankly asked me, "*What job do you want to do?*"

Based largely on my childhood experiences, I replied, "*I like fixing things, I like working outside, and I want to be around jets.*"

With a wide grin growing across his narrow face, he said, "*You want to be a crew chief!*"

Outwardly displaying my ignorance, I said, "*Great, what's a crew chief?*"

He explained the crew chief is the maintainer who "owns" the aircraft and coordinates all maintenance efforts to ensure flight-worthy status. That all sounded cool to me, so I signed up on the spot. *Opportunity.*

I departed for basic training knowing nothing of the transformation about to take place. In just six short weeks, the Air Force changed me from "Paul the cotton farmer" to "Airman White," complete with the training and discipline required to succeed as an enlisted airman in the military. Graduation from basic training meant shipping away to another Air Force Base (AFB) for technical school to learn crew chief basics. Randomly sitting in a restaurant one evening in the spring of 1997, I met a smoking hot blonde named Katie, who would eventually become my wife and mother to my three sons. *Opportunity.*

Following technical school, the Air Force sent me to Tyndall AFB outside Panama City, Florida, for my first assignment. For the next three years, I grew as a crew chief, got married, had my first son, and earned a reputation as someone willing to do hard things to get better and get the job done. Less than 90 days after my three-year Air Force anniversary, I tested for staff sergeant and scored high enough to earn promotion. In less than four years, I became a non-commissioned officer (NCO), a supervisor and was working toward becoming a seven-level craftsman maintainer. *Opportunity.*

By this time, my wife and son and I had moved to Elmendorf AFB, Alaska. One random day driving in the back gate, I saw a small rectangular brown sign that had an arrow pointing to the right and the words EDUCATION OFFICE printed in big white block letters. I slammed on the brakes and walked into the office that would change my life forever. After explaining to the attendant that I was thinking about going to school, she asked what I did for the Air Force. She took my information and sent me downstairs to the Embry-Riddle Aeronautical University office. I was not in the Embry-Riddle office more than 30 minutes and returned to the main desk with a plan to get my Bachelor of Science in Aeronautics. *Opportunity.*

I was poised to finish my last semester at Embry-Riddle in spring 2003, six months after my second son was born. I was also up for my next promotion, technical sergeant, the rank widely known in the Air

Force enlisted promotion system as the hardest rank to earn. Despite the odds, I studied hard, made the rank by a good margin, and earned a 4.0 GPA in four college classes, all while juggling home life with two young sons and a full-time job. *Opportunity.*

Finished with my bachelor's degree, I decided to keep pressing towards a master's degree. With all the coursework complete in the summer of 2004, I applied to Officer Training School almost on a dare. Two weeks after my third son was born, I received a call from my commander congratulating me on selection to Officer Training School. He also informed me I was chosen to be a navigator, and after a few Google searches, I realized I could earn a fighter weapons systems officer (WSO, pronounced whiz-o) spot, so I set my goal. Some of the best advice I got during my transition from enlisted to officer was from my maintenance officer's husband, a fighter pilot in our squadron. He grabbed me in a headlock after a few beers and told me, *"Just be the best at everything and you'll get whatever you want."* *Opportunity.*

Two years later, I completed flight school at the top of my class and was headed to Seymour Johnson AFB, North Carolina, for the F-15E Strike Eagle basic qualification course. I had earned my selection as a fighter WSO. I flew Strike Eagles for many years, but in the fall of 2015, I knew my time in the Air Force was coming to an end. I was comfortable at my current assignment, qualified in everything I could be, and my family was in a good spot to grow and flourish.

I wanted to stay and retire, but in October that year, I received a one-off assignment to Luke AFB, Arizona, to fly F-16s with the Republic of Singapore Air Force. They were in desperate need of an instructor WSO, and I was the only one qualified and available in the timeframe they needed. I could have rejected the assignment and retired where I was, but after a week-long discussion with my wife, we decided to move to Arizona. *Opportunity.*

I retired from the Air Force after that assignment in 2018. Following retirement from active duty, I took a job at the base as a subject matter expert and built a training program still in use today. That job opened a door for me to become an F-35 instructor. A WSO, straight from the cotton field, is a civilian fighter pilot instructor on the F-35, the Air Force's premier fighter aircraft, all from taking advantage of opportunity.

America is the land of opportunity. If you have a good attitude, pay attention and give maximum effort, you can redefine and reach well beyond your potential. Even if you don't know exactly what you want to do in your life, give due diligence, work hard at every endeavor and keep your eyes on the horizon for the next opportunity. You never know who is watching and what doors will open. You don't always have to be the shiniest penny. Sometimes, you just need to be a penny when they need a penny. Your version of the American Dream is alive and well if you are willing to do what it takes to achieve.

Begin now by creating and taking advantage of opportunity.

"BE 1 OF 5"

"You are the average of the 5 people
you spend the most time with."
– Jim Rohn

Immediately, you probably thought about the 5 people you hang out with most. Turn the phrase on its head and take a different perspective. Look at it from others' points of view. True, they are "1 of your 5," but you are one of theirs as well. My challenge to you is to look inward and seek self-improvement for your benefit and of those around you. You never know who is watching, so focus on the things you can control and your own mind-body-soul balance, and you will, in turn, raise their average in the process as 1 of their 5.

Be 1 of 5.

Outwardly display an image of a person not afraid to do hard things to get better. Look for and take advantage of opportunities, and always strive to be a better person than you were yesterday. American society may be divided more than ever, but if every American will focus on being a better "1 of 5," we all raise our averages. And America will continue to be a nation every other country envies.

Andrew Hibbard

Andrew Hibbard is a 10-year veteran of the United States Air Force. His passion for patriotism and leadership began at an early age based on lessons learned with the Boy Scouts. After high school, he joined his local volunteer Fire Department, and later enlisted as a firefighter with the USAF Fire Department.

His path to pursue excellence earned him the coveted "Honor Graduate" ribbon from Air Force Basic Training, along with the "Top Graduate" award from the Department of Defense Fire Academy, along with two Air Force Meritorious Service Medals.

After proudly serving his country, Andrew is now proudly serving his community offering paid consulting services to insurance agents wanting to build a 7-figure business. He and his wife, Lyndsey, along with their kids and dog, live in Akron, NY. Learn more about Andrew at:

https://Andrew-Hibbard.com

Chapter #2

A LETTER TO CHARLIE
(MY FIRSTBORN DAUGHTER)

I'm not sure how old you'll be when you get around to reading this, if ever. I'm not naïve to the fact that much of my life so far has been like much of everybody's life, of little interest to anyone but me, but one thing seems to stand out as something worth sharing. Something of importance that you should carry with you for the rest of your life. A sort of north star that will always right your ship if you are led astray. So, please, I hope you will stick with me long enough here to learn this valuable life lesson. I hope it will all make sense to you someday.

While I sit and write this letter, I find myself contemplating what the purpose behind my message will be. I'm not very introspective and tend to be too busy living life to seriously ponder the meaning of it. But this process has forced me to slow down and think, and I have given this parenting thing a great deal of thought.

You see, there is a questioning of conservative and traditional family values that's beginning to change the current culture across the country. It seems like younger parents and new generations aren't sure an appreciation and love of America is the right thing to teach. Mom and I have struggled to embrace this change.

It is troubling for us to think about what kind of country it seems you will grow up in. I hope we are not making a mistake trying to teach you to be a strong, independent individual with an ambitious attitude and a bit of grit.

The world around you may someday look much different than the world as you know it today. Life will become hard. And, as you pursue more meaningful things, everything will become even harder.

Small things will become big.
Uncomplicated things will become complicated.

Much of this will be out of your control. Everything worth doing will undoubtedly become more and more of a challenge as you get older. But here's what I want you to remember: "*America was built on being of service to others.*"

That might be the most important and impactful information I can impart in you. A lesson I had to learn over time, not instantly.

You may not remember this, but when you just started to get a little confidence walking (well, actually weeble-wobbling), I would bring you to my office, just the two of us, so we could spend more time together (and give Mom a much-deserved break). You always waddled from room to room, opening every drawer within your reach, looking for that teeny, tiny, red, white and blue American Flag pin I kept. You loved that pin. "*Daddy, I have? I have, daddy?*" you would say. As often as I can remember, you had it proudly pinned on every shirt you wore.

Truthfully, you probably only liked it because it was shiny. Or maybe just because it was mine, and it reminded you of me, but the meaning of what that American Flag pin represents is far greater than you may ever realize. And I don't think I ever really explained the importance of it to you and why I wear it every day.

It was actually on the last day that I wore my U.S. Air Force uniform when, for the first time, I felt like I knew what the uniform stood for—what the American Flag patch, sewn onto my right shoulder, symbolized.

You weren't much past two weeks old at the time, and Mom and I had been having a lot of tough talks late at night, after you were asleep, about the future of the family. I'm curious to know what you remember hearing at the top of the stairs? (Yes, we knew that you would sneak out of bed and listen in on the adult conversations being had.)

The writing on the wall was clear about creating a more profitable civilian career and walking away from what we felt was a limiting military life. We had two choices to make, and really only one made sense: Stay in the Air Force or get out.

Fast forward 6 months down the road, and I am standing, heels together with toes spread 45 degrees apart, rigid like a pole, arms glued to my sides, in the Fire Department truck bay. It's a hot, humid, July day, and the entire squadron was just called to attention for our Commander's Change of Command ceremony.

There are a lot of typical customs and courtesies to these types of things. Most of the details will only be significant to me, and very insignificant to you, but what you need to know is when the incoming commander finished his acceptance speech, he asked to play a new rendition of Lee Greenwood's "God Bless the USA," recently re-recorded with the U.S. Air Force. The songs opening lines start with:

I LOVE AMERICA

"If tomorrow all the things were gone,
I'd worked for all my life,
And I had to start again,
with just my children and my wife,
I'd thank my lucky stars,
to be living here today,
Where the flag still stands for freedom,
and they can't take that away."

I'll tell you, when I heard those words, my heart started pounding. I could feel my face getting flushed. My ears hot to the touch. And tears just streamed down my face.

Now, you may not believe what I just said about the tears. I know I've always told you I've never felt that crying solves much. There's really no point to it in my mind. But I couldn't hold them back.

You see, Mom and I had come to the agreement that going all in on our family business would provide us many more valuable opportunities moving forward, and the time had come where the Air Force no longer made sense to keep making it a priority.

It was surreal to hear Lee Greenwood's song lyrics. They seemed sung to me personally. My stomach was sinking with the thought about tomorrow's truth when everything I worked for all my life would be gone, and I would be starting again, with just my children and my wife. I began to question who I would need to become, for who I have been, I would no longer be.

I started playing back my past and the particular path of stepping stones taken to arrive at this one meaningful moment: joining Boy Scouts early in childhood, working as a town lifeguard, signing up with our local volunteer fire department, and enlisting with the Air Force Fire Department. It was with these flashbacks, these memories, that helped me remember what I've done, so I'd know who I am—a man of service.

But something interesting happened. I soon saw that behind the shroud of service was actually something quite selfish I had never known while living each of these former lives.

As young as I can remember, I loved camping, being outdoors, the woods, and nature. And Boy Scouts promised the opportunity for more outdoor adventure. Joining was a purely selfish reason to pursue my own self-interest. But, over time, as I progressed in rank and promoted on my way to earning Eagle Scout, I became indoctrinated into the importance of serving others and living by the Scout Slogan, "Do a Good Turn Daily."

Lifeguarding was simply a need for a summer job and a way to earn my own money. Volunteer fire-fighting was a way to do something "cool." And enlisting in the Air Force Fire Department was a shortcut to a full-time job.

But here's the thing, Charlie, each and every time I have started something in pursuit of pure self-interest, they have always, without fail, ended up becoming something much bigger than myself. And the common thread woven between all of these life chapters has been, and continues to be, wearing with me the symbol of service, the American Flag. On my scout uniform, on my lifeguard trunks, on my fire-fighter turnout gear, and on my Air Force duty uniform.

That's why I make it a point to wear that shiny American Flag pin every day now. The same pin that you loved to look for, high and low, all those early mornings when we were at the office together, just you and me. I wear that pin as a daily reminder to constantly strive to be of service to others.

I hope you take time to find a way to be of service to others as you begin to leave your legacy in this world, and take your God-given talents and skills to make a meaningful impact in a positive way.

Your efforts may start out as a selfish desire or in search of self-interest, and that's okay; just make sure they morph into something more meaningful and become bigger than yourself. Take these tips with you as you do great things:

- Remember how resourceful you can be seeking solutions to your own problems, and look to leverage the opportunity to offer the same solution to others.

- Remind yourself of your resilience as you face adversity and need to overcome challenges. It's not an if, but when.

- Remain resolute to the reasons why you choose to pursue the path you purposely pick. You will certainly face critics and your convictions with be tested. Often, the mass majority may not share your same wants and wishes, and if you don't stand for something, you will fall for anything. It may matter most who is in the company you keep.

Big problems can be solved with small solutions, but only if you recognize it begins with being of service to others. I love you.

P.S. Remember what Dr. Seuss said, "*Unless someone like you cares a whole awful lot, nothing is going to get better. It's not.*"

SERVICE TO OTHERS CAN BE SELF-SERVING, TOO

What if you knew that most modern conveniences you use, like, and enjoy happened only out of pure selfishness? Would it take away from making your life easier or simpler? Here are some quick examples:

- The wheel ("I'm tired of walking").
- The bike ("I need to go faster than walking").
- The car ("I need to go faster than a bike").
- The airplane ("I need to go faster than a car").

Self-interest can be a great motivator. Both good and bad, I'll admit, but for the most part, we're all better today because someone else before us was just a little selfish about something.

What's wrong with that, if serving your own self -interest can serve others in a meaningful way at the same time?

I challenge readers to find small ways you can serve yourself better. When you serve yourself best, you can begin to serve your family best. When your family is served best, you can serve your community best. And when our communities are served best, our country will be served best. That's the only way we keep America great.

Tracey Brown

Tracey Brown is a veteran of the U.S. Coast Guard. Her journey into understanding how our "mind is set" was born from literal flames due to severe burns at the age of eight as well as the trauma associated with four years of doing Search and Rescue and Marine Safety.

Her first book, *Rescue to Recovery*, is her story of navigating over 30 years of undiagnosed PTSD. She came to understand that injuries to our soul need support to heal just like physical injuries do, and this set the stage for the next chapter of her life as an author and speaker. Tracey's passion is to share her life experiences and her belief in the power of the mind to create our best life. Tracey is a mental fitness instructor with Polk Institute, a two-time #1 best-selling author and an international award-winning speaker on Mindset, Excellence and Fun. To learn more about Tracey, visit:

https://RescueToRecovery.com

Chapter 3

AMERICA: WHERE DREAMS STILL COME TRUE

Ever since I was a little girl, my mom told me that I could do anything that I set my mind to. She taught me that even though she had to fight for so many things as a woman, with the advent of women's rights and Title IX, I as a young woman, could do anything because we live in America. She instilled in me the understanding that being an American citizen was unique from all other countries because we are free to choose what we do and how we live. My dad was a pilot in the U.S. Navy and proudly served during the Korean War, and he also instilled that same sense of pride in being an American.

To this day, when I say I am an American, that pride is still as strong as ever. After serving for four years in the U.S. Coast Guard as a small boat swimmer and crew member in San Francisco, CA, (before there was a school for swimmers) and a Marine Safety Inspector, that pride is accompanied by a greater understanding of the sacrifices made to create and maintain this great land.

When people from faraway places hear the word America, it stirs up hope. It conjures up the idea that anything is possible. Millions of people give up everything just for the chance to come here. They come here for a new life, for opportunity, to bring dreams to reality—for freedom—freedom many of us were fortunate to be born into.

America is absolutely beautiful; I have had the great pleasure of traveling through much of this country. It's not just the beauty of her land and seascapes from coast to coast and the truly unlimited resources within her borders, but perhaps the greatest of her resources are the innovative and creative people that naturally emerge from this free society.

Our freedoms, our rights, are given to us by our Creator. Our right to liberty and the pursuit of happiness perpetuates an innovative spirit and creative mindset. What peace we have that we can wake up without fear of a tyrant coming to take our hopes and dreams away as it was in the days this nation was becoming the light upon the hill that she is.

I'm a fan of American history. We have a rich, and yes, very diverse history. The older I get, the more I realize how young we are as a nation in light of other nations. In my humble opinion, it seems that as our country was being "born," those that were in attendance at that time learned an awful lot about what they wanted in a nation and certainly what they didn't want.

I believe that our Constitution is one of the most amazing contracts ever written. Is it perfect? No. Is it amazing and absolutely brilliant? Yes. Does it create a country where you can start with absolutely nothing and bring forth into existence anything that you can imagine? ABSOLUTELY! As long as we are willing to put our head, our hearts and our hands to it, we can bring it about. The older I get, the more I believe this to be true.

Our mindset, regarding what it is that we so choose to do, is everything. As the great saying goes, *"Those who think they can and those who think they can't are both usually right."* This is no truer here in the USA than anywhere in the world. THE land of opportunity; if you can think it, you can be it. There is nowhere else on this earth that you can say that without question.

This country is unique from all others because we are a republic built BY the people—FOR the people. What bold imagination and conviction inspired those that envisioned this great nation! Our freedoms are not given to us by those that we elect: our freedoms are given to us by God and God alone. Those we elect merely implement the will of the people. It is by the everyday person of old with their understanding of individual liberties and God-given rights that this nation was born. This country was literally birthed from the chains of tyranny.

The expression and application of these rights is the backbone of commerce, which perpetuates more innovation and sustainability. With this comes responsibility to DO our best, BE our best and re-spect ALL peoples and the precious land that we have inherited.

As a member of the United States Coast Guard, I took great pride in taking the oath to protect and serve and to uphold our amazing Constitution, and even though my service was completed years ago, now as a veteran, I take pride in the fact that I had that opportunity to serve.

I believe that every now and then we need to look back at our history to regain vision of our future. Those that went before us to forge this great nation were not only amazing and brilliant, but they were also surprisingly young, many in their 20's and 30's (young to me now that I am older ☺). And so, I share something I came across that each time I read, it reignites my pride, joy and understanding of the significance of this nation we call home.

A quote from a pamphlet called *Common Sense* written by Thomas Paine was read to the American people by John Adams in 1776, and he read, *"The cause of America is in great measure the cause of all mankind."* It was an astonishing and inspiring claim about the fate of thirteen infant colonies on the edge of the world, noted by another author. *"The sun never shone on a cause of greater worth. Tis not the affair of a city, a county, a province, or a kingdom; but of a continent—of at least one-eighth part of the habitable globe. Tis not the concern of the day, year, or an age; posterity will be more or less affected, even to the end of time, by the proceedings now."*

Those proceedings were the Declaration of Independence.

Looking back at what the authors of this contract wrote and what they did to bring this about is beyond inspiring. It creates a desire in me to do my part beyond my military service, but perhaps as important, in my daily service to others in how I "show up" and the choices I make to make the world around me a better place.

Jim Rohn, a great business philosopher said, *"Take more time working on yourself than you do on your business."*

His premise was that in working on ourselves, we will create the character needed to create a great business. I am a hopeful optimist. I believe that if each of us strive to be the best version of ourselves, if we make a conscious decision each day to do what it takes to create our best life, we will be more joyful, more vibrant and more encouraging to others. I believe that as more and more of us choose to find the joy of life in our life, we can create a better world and further the cause of this great nation. Being our best and doing our best is a great service each of us can do for our communities, if we so choose.

MY BEST LIFE CHALLENGE

So, in the spirit of the great Jim Rohn, I have a challenge. The way it works is simple. Ask yourself a very serious but truly unselfish question:

WHAT DO I WANT?

Really take time with yourself for yourself. When it comes to your family, relationships, health, your business, your fun..., ask yourself, "*What do I want?*"

And on the heels of that, ask yourself, "*What am I willing to do to get it, to bring it about?*" Ethically, legally and morally, of course ☺.

Most people take more time planning a vacation than they do planning their life, retirement or legacy. So, take the time, take some hours or a day to really contemplate what you want. Do this with each area of your life, and revisit it often.

I believe that because of our brilliant nation built on innovation, inspiration and perspiration, each one of us can not only pursue happiness but also achieve it, and in doing so, we continue the cause of this beautiful nation.

Jeff Arnold

Jeff Arnold is a veteran of the United States Army, Oklahoma Army national Guard and Arizona Army national Guard. He is the author of six books with four of them holding the highly coveted title of Best Seller. After his Army experience, Jeff pursued drama, stage acting and comedy in Hollywood. The Universe quickly revealed to him that a Star of the Stage, he may not be, but the gift of gab combined with writing, and what others have termed, "Kissed by the Blarney Stone," he most certainly possesses.

Jeff writes, speaks and educates listeners on the subjects of money, happiness, religion, patriotism, and that sexiest of all industries: insurance. Having bought more than 40 insurance brokerages, two insurance companies, and served as CEO over three firms, he is now focused on giving back to his local community and telling stories about how he loves America.

https://JeffArnold.com

Chapter 4

THE AMERICA
OF MY YOUTH

March 11, 1987
2:33 PM
Phoenix, Arizona

America Loses a Son

The mood in the room is somber as I slip into the end row, last seat of the pew. The only sounds are sniffles and an occasional labored gasp for a breath or guttural sigh by females in attendance. For many of the men in the room, there is a stoic, hard-faced, clenched-jaw look with a visible sound of loud swallowing to push back emotions and the inevitable wiping of a tear sliding down their cheeks.

The sermon is over, and I sit alone, the last person to leave the viewing area. I make my way to the grave site where the air smells of newly tossed dirt.

The sun warms my "numb from the pain body," and the burial begins.

My best friend and Army buddy is lying in a now-closed casket and gently lowered down into his final resting place. I am overcome with the finality of, "*We will never again enjoy a beer, never create another memory, never watch the Steelers win or lose, never shine boots together and never will he meet my future wife or children.*" It's a shitty thing that when it comes to best friends, only one of you will attend the other's funeral.

Anyone with military experience knows what happens next. "Taps," begins to play:

Here at rest
With the Blest
For his Country, he did his best
Put the flag upon his breast
Comrade rest

Today, of course, the song and the words hit very different. The music pierces my ears, and I am engulfed with more emotional pain and physical hurt than at any other time in my life. Have you ever had to sit silently, listening to "Taps" being played while your best friend is buried? I can tell you that the pause between each note is an absolute eternity.

Have you ever witnessed firsthand the gut-wrenching pain of watching a mother being presented the American Flag while simultaneously burying her son? I can tell you, there cannot possibly be a pain greater than that of a parent burying a child. Can you picture her with the now-folded flag clutched in her grasp, receiving a salute from the honor guard? The bugle playing "Taps" decrescendos to its end as the rifle detail fires shots in unison. With each shot, there is an echo followed by a crackling sound filling the air.

I struggle to empty the heartache by a clandestinely released muffled exhale, mouth slightly open in an O shape, trying not to interrupt the silence or take away the moment of honoring America's latest lost son.

May the memory of United States Army Chief Warrant Officer CW2 David O. Barr be a reminder of those who willingly pay the ultimate price in the name of a country, a flag, a belief in eternal freedom and the protection of that freedom by brave men and women who have, do, and will sacrifice everything for those ideals.

A Family with a Deep Legacy of Service

While my best friend, Dave Barr, is a constant memory, especially on Memorial Day and Veterans Day, I should also like to share about a family that has a deep legacy of military service, and I could readily fill an entire book with their service history.

My grandparents got married literally days before my grandfather was shipped out to the South Pacific to fight in WWII. He often told me stories about serving with the Navy and made sure that all his grandchildren understood the horrors of war but was also deeply convicted that all should serve both God and the Flag. *"Man, he loved America, like nobody else I ever met."*

My stepfather, the man who sacrificed greatly to raise me and my siblings, was a career Chief Warrant Officer CW5. I don't think the Army had a helicopter he didn't fly while serving his country for more than three decades. He raised us by being a constant example of what the values of "**Duty, Honor, Country**" mean. His parental guidance led me to enlist days after graduating high school.

My brother serves as a command sergeant major and has represented this country in nearly all theaters of combat since 1986. He has missed more family events than most could imagine, ranging from children's first steps, proms, graduations, grandchildren being born—all in the name of selfless devotion to the United States of America.

My own journey in the United States Army just happened to coincide with a newly organized Special Operations Battalion created for counterterrorism and Spec Ops. The unit was created after the failed hostage rescue mission in Iran. The Pentagon leadership implied whatever the costs, whatever we do, we can never have another Desert One. While other Soldiers served in daylight, every single night we conducted exercises with modified night vision goggles and a seemingly limitless budget of whatever equipment we needed. It is also in this unit that the United States lost several exemplary Soldiers; I lost three good comrades and witnessed the burial of my best friend.

The America of My Youth

I grew up in a *flag-raising, gather round the circle, hold hands and sing American songs* family in western Kentucky. Each ceremony would also be followed by a prayer as many in my family were ministers, preachers, and men of the cloth.

Every Fourth of July for as long as I can remember, (and yes, still to this day) members of our family make a pilgrimage back to Kentucky from Arizona, Florida, Indiana, Tennessee, Germany and Poland. We descend upon a tiny row house in Versailles, Kentucky, where my 97-year-old grandmother still lives, to celebrate family, faith, country and partake in Fourth of July weekend events and reunions.

These events are filled with fireworks, cornhole contests, and a myriad of competitive games, but always—without fail—on the Fourth of July, a flag will be raised, a salute will be made, members of our family who have served in past wars from WWII, Korea, Vietnam, Iraq, and Afghanistan will be honored and thanked, and a circle will be formed with hands held, patriotic songs sung—ending with "God Bless America" and closed with a prayer.

A New and Different America Is Emerging

I, quite candidly, had never been exposed to any anti-America sentiment before social media. Somehow, post adoption of me downloading and using social media, my feed would repeat messages of an America that I could not fathom others believed to be true. There is a consistent barrage of vitriolic, hate-filled, bigoted, rejoicing in flag burning, "America was never great" chants, kneeling during the "National Anthem" actions that turn my stomach.

Those voices seemingly grow louder the further down the age chart one goes, and it distresses me that many of our youth are fully indoctrinated with a slew of anti-American statements without an alternative input source that discusses all the wonderful things and opportunities that makes America the GREAT country I believe she is.

A Longing for the Past

While it is true that I, like so many older Americans, long for the America of yesteryear, I also know it to be true that the old memories of the America we grew up with are, in fact, in the past. And that version of America is most likely "*not coming back*."

Still, there is much to celebrate regarding our future. The beauty of America is and has always been that each of us is allowed our own beliefs. The America I love is filled with people who believe different than me, worship a different God than me, and have distinctly different viewpoints than me, but in the end, the variety of viewpoints each of us holds is what makes America so GREAT. She is a giant melting pot of individuality, opinionated differences, unique customs and norms, all allowed to flourish under the stars and stripes.

AMERICA:
A Grand Experiment Like No Other

This glorious experiment in unparalleled freedoms, the diversity of beliefs, thought, and religion is unlike any other country in the world. Indeed, I submit to you that each of us can possess alternative or differing opinions and still live harmoniously.

The growing division can be halted and even reversed if we seek to understand, adopt and practice love, forgiveness and acceptance. Years ago, a 17th century poet penned the words:

"A man convinced against his will,
is of the same opinion still."

Neither I nor you are going to convince others that the America we want is the right America. America is what she is. And to each that believe in her, she IS THE AMERICA they want. It is this America that my family has and continues to fight for, that Dave willingly gave his life for. It is for this America that I pray. It is for this America that generations to come will hopefully continue to stand for, believe in and defend. It is for this America that I should like to present you with a final thought.

The entire world is a better place because 246 years ago, a handful of men pledged their lives, fortunes and liberty for the belief in these 36 words.

"We hold these truths to be self-evident,
that all men are created equal,
that they are endowed by their Creator with certain
unalienable rights,
that among these are life, liberty and the pursuit of
happiness."

Man, I sure do love America.

WHAT DOES AMERICA NEED FROM YOU?

As so many of this book's authors have aptly stated, there is much to love about America. A famous statesman once remarked, "Ask not what your country can do for you, but rather what can you do for your country." This illuminating statement challenged generations of Americans and shifted mindsets from an expectation mentality to one of contribution.

We need to ask ourselves these types of direct questions once more: *How can you and I give back to America? How do we teach future generations to fall in love with America?*

My succinct compilation of values that should be embraced by future generations to love America are: Stand for the flag; kneel to your God; reinstate the Pledge of Allegiance in our schools; transfer the knowledge of "*Duty, Honor, Country*" to our youth; and begin all of these at your own dinner table.

Go forth and replace your dreams of a better America with a plan of action. Start where you are. Begin in your own kitchen. Dive in.

American needs you—now more than ever.

Brandi Barnard "BB" King

"BB" King is a wife, mother, military veteran, and professional airline pilot. She and her husband, Daniel "Rabbi" King, also a military veteran, now fly for major airlines. They currently live in San Antonio, Texas, with their teenage sons. When they aren't at football or basketball games, their family tries to spend as much time as possible enjoying God's creation deep in the heart of Texas (Hill Country).

BB spent almost twenty years serving as an officer and pilot in the United States Air Force. She continues to uphold her oath to support and defend the Constitution of the United States of America and the God-given liberties it protects. Her love of Christ, family, and country is demonstrated through her bold proclamation of the truth and unwavering commitment to stand against tyranny and the suppression of freedom. To learn more about BB's love of America, visit:

https://BBKing4Freedom.com

Chapter 5

BRAVEHEART LOVE

I had left Chicago, Illinois, and returned to my hometown of San Antonio, Texas, to visit my parents and finish planning my wedding, which was less than two months away. We were sitting in the living room, drinking coffee and talking while the television provided some background noise. Our joy-filled smiles and hopeful hearts were overcome by darkness, confusion, and shock with the sights and sounds that came from the news. We did not know then what we know now.

The date 9/11 would never be thought of the same. After finally understanding that Americans had been attacked by enemies desiring to kill innocent people, it became incredibly difficult for me to concentrate on our upcoming celebration. I was so full of righteous anger that I felt like I was channeling the spirit of William Wallace, played by Mel Gibson, in the 1995 movie, *Braveheart.*

I was driven to put sacrificial <u>love</u> into action as a means of providing justice and protection for our country and our way of life. I wanted to do anything I could to ensure terrorists, tyrants, and oppressors knew they did not have any authority over Americans nor the right to usurp our God-given <u>freedom</u> through the use of fear tactics. Following the horrific evil of 9/11, I eagerly swore an oath to support and defend the Constitution of the United States of America. This single day changed my life vector forever; I became committed to commissioning as an officer and becoming a pilot in the United States Air Force.

Webster's Dictionary defines <u>love</u> as a strong affection for another arising out of personal ties, an attraction based on sexual desire, or affection based on admiration. Scripture, which helped guide and direct our forefathers in writing the Constitution, defines <u>love</u> as a dedicated, sacrificial commitment that is based in action and intended for the good of others. (Read 1 John 3:16 & 18.)

The Bible, the most widely available read and referenced literature in the 18th Century Constitutional Convention era, tells us to <u>love</u> God with all our hearts and to <u>love</u> others as ourselves. (Read Luke 10:27.)

The Bible also acknowledges that we are <u>free</u> to choose to adhere to or diverge from following the law, knowing that the scales of justice always find equilibrium. (Read Proverbs 21:15.)

<u>Freedom</u> is a result of sacrificial <u>love</u>. *"It is for freedom that Christ set us <u>free</u>. Stand firm, then, and do not let yourselves be burdened again by the yoke of slavery."* Galatians 5:1 (NIV)

We are never to waste sacrificial <u>love</u> and its costly gift of <u>freedom</u> by returning to bondage. Evildoers use fear as a weapon to coerce us to give up our <u>freedom</u> and reenter bondage.

The opening paragraph of the Declaration of Independence asserts our <u>freedom</u> birthright perfectly. During the 1787 summer convention in Philadelphia (City of Brotherly <u>Love</u>), the framers of our Constitution understood this Biblical principle of <u>freedom</u>-giving <u>love</u>, and they knew that our God-inspired law of the land must guarantee *"the blessings of liberty"* for all people and provide protection of the enumerable, unalienable rights that are *"endowed by the Creator."* Our Founding Fathers understood that such <u>freedom</u> could only be protected if a government derived powers solely from the consent of the governed.

God's <u>love</u>, shared through His Word, can be seen in our Constitution through phrases such as *"We hold these truths to be self-evident, that all men are created equal, that they are endowed by their Creator with certain unalienable rights, that among these are life, liberty and the pursuit of happiness."*

These great men often referenced Biblical teachings as essential to the founding of the United States of America and its governing documents. Benjamin Franklin quoted 14 Bible verses in 14 sentences during one of his impromptu speeches at the Constitutional Convention.

Alexander Hamilton stated, *"The sacred rights of mankind are not to be rummaged for among old parchments or musty records. They are written, as with a sunbeam, in the whole volume of human nature, by the hand of the Divinity itself, and can never be erased or obscured by mortal power."*

The aforementioned sunbeam written Scripture says, *"And now these three remain: faith, hope, and <u>love</u>. But the greatest of these is <u>love</u>."* 1 Corinthians 13:13 (NIV)

You must see <u>love</u> through the lens of the Bible rather than through that of Disney, or you will never believe me when I tell you that Sir William Wallace (Braveheart) was full of <u>love</u>. Real <u>love</u> has nothing to do with physical attraction, being nice, tolerance of behavior, or feelings. <u>Love</u> does not necessarily protect people physically or emotionally, but rather, <u>love</u> focuses on the ultimate good of another.

We are called to <u>love</u> others by providing swift justice for a crime (wrongdoing) even when it is difficult or creates discomfort. (Read Ecclesiastes 8:11.)

Parents understand this type of Braveheart <u>love</u>. In Ephesians 6:4, we read that we should <u>love</u> our children by teaching and disciplining them. Proverbs 27:17 tells us not to spare the rod. Because of <u>love,</u> we are to keep others accountable to the law. We are told to <u>love</u> others not by enabling their self-destructive behavior by giving them sustenance, but rather by teaching and helping them find sustainable work. (Read 2 Thessalonians 3:10.)

These same principles are easily discernable as foundational to our Constitution. The 39 signatories did not design the Constitution to oppose <u>love</u>, but rather, they designed it to promote natural order and enable <u>love through justice</u> for the good of *We the People*.

Sir William "Braveheart" Wallace demonstrated sacrificial <u>love</u> through <u>justice</u>. He was driven to bring justice against the English for their longstanding assault on <u>freedom,</u> as evidenced by the abuse and murder of the Scottish people. In his righteous anger, Wallace offered forgiveness and redemption through consequences and justice. He offered his enemies a choice of reconciliation through repentance or through retribution:

"Lower your flags and march straight back to England, stopping at every home you pass by to beg forgiveness for a hundred years of theft, rape, and murder. Do that and your men shall live. Do it not, and every one of you will die today."

Why did he specifically mandate repentance and acceptance of consequences for violations of law and natural order? I believe he did so out of <u>love</u> and out of the respect for the <u>freedom</u> of all mankind. Braveheart also inspired his fellow countrymen to fight for <u>freedom</u>. Remember his words:

"Fight and you might die. Run and you would live, at least a while. And then, dying in your beds many years later, would you be willing to trade all the days from that day for one chance to go back and tell the tyrannical enemy that they may take your lives, but they will never take your <u>freedom</u>?"

So, how does Braveheart fit into my personal story of upholding laws/standards, <u>freedom,</u> and <u>love</u>? After visiting more countries than I can count, I have seen lawlessness, oppression, and the resulting poverty. Evil knows no end if <u>freedom</u> is not continually preserved through law and order by those of us capable of exhibiting Braveheart <u>love</u>. I have landed in countries where emaciated men, women, and children hung on airport perimeter fences just to get a glimpse of my airplane with the U.S. flag tail flash.

They waited eagerly to wave at me—the <u>freedom</u>-fighting American—as I exited the airplane.

I'd walk over, smile, shake hands, and give them patches off my uniform. These people, not even American citizens, thanked me wholeheartedly for defending <u>freedom</u> and providing hope. They'd point at the U.S. flag patch and then to their hearts. It renewed my spirit every time I encountered such raw gratitude and respect for the continual pursuit and defense of <u>freedom</u>. It reminded me that America's power resides with *We the People*. We are called to decentralize power and implement equal justice for all. The Constitution, serving as the highest law of the land, allows us to maintain order, fight corruption, oppression, and ensure <u>freedom</u> for our nation, which serves as "*a light to the world, a city on the hill*" for the greater good of the world.

Serving in the military has taught me that <u>freedom</u> is dependent upon the Braveheart <u>love</u> that propels us to sacrifice self (comfort, sleep, family time, home life, and sometimes life) to uphold the Constitution and the God-given liberty it protects. We must all continue to carry the torch of <u>freedom</u>.

From its birth, America has been full of Braveheart <u>love</u>; it is what has sustained our <u>liberty</u> and <u>justice</u> for all, for over 235 years. It is woven into the fabric of who we are.

The majority of the 56 signers of the Declaration of Independence were tortured, lost loved ones, lost fortunes, or lost their own lives in the pursuit of securing our independence/<u>freedom</u>. These men embodied *sacrificial <u>love</u> in action and brave hearts, all in the name of <u>freedom</u> through <u>justice</u>*.

We often imagine that <u>love</u> turns a blind eye or just lets things be, that <u>love</u> ignores things when they go wrong. This is not <u>love</u>; rather, it is indifference. True <u>love</u>, Braveheart <u>love</u>, and Biblical <u>love</u> include judgment. Judgement and justice provide the restoration of order. <u>Love</u> cares too much to be indifferent towards the destruction of our lives from our bondage and slavery to sin. There is no <u>love</u> without justice; the Bible tells me so.

No matter our surname, skin color, gender, zip code, vaccination status, or from what land or tribe we originally hailed, *We the People* are called to be united, bravehearted, <u>freedom-loving</u>, <u>justice-serving</u> Americans. One nation under God.

This is why I <u>love</u> America!

Resources: online.hillsdale.edu; prageru.com; truthforhealth.org; Holy Bible App

CHANNEL YOUR INNER BRAVEHEART!

I challenge you to live out the American motto, "In God We Trust," by first committing to regularly reading the Bible, then the Constitution of the United States, The U.S. Bill of Rights, and the U.S. Declaration of Independence. To do so will hone your understanding of the God-given freedom that led to the law upon which our country was founded, and it will give you the courage and strength to live out "Braveheart love."

Of utmost importance, we need to share the Bible and our nation's founding documents with our children. It is imperative that we continually secure liberty by committing to love-based action, by sacrificing time, worldly comfort—or fear of discomfort—in standing up against tyranny and totalitarianism, which aim to divide and conquer us. Focus on freedom over fear. We must all continue to support and defend our Constitution to ensure those that came before us did not labor and die in vain. Remember, love is sacrifice in action. I challenge you to work hard at maintaining our founders' Biblical worldview, embody "Braveheart love," and uphold the law through justice in order to preserve our great American "F-R-E-E-D-O-M!"

Jody Gatchell

Jody Gatchell started his career growing up on a family farm in Minnesota. This background of hard work and responsibility was the foundation that built the rest his of military and professional career. Helping his great grandma, grandpa, and dad with everyday tasks on the farm was the perfect way to mold him for future endeavors.

Joining the Army a couple years out of high school was the start of his journey into the world on his own. During his seven years as a military policeman, he was stationed in White Sands Missile Range, Mannheim Germany, and Fort Benning, Georgia.

His career after the Army led him to become the owner of an automotive collision repair business. Starting the business with just two individuals, it grew to a staff of 15. During his time as the owner, Jody and his crew donated ten vehicles to individuals and non-profits in his community.

Chapter #6

A LIFETIME OF
OPPORTUNITIES

Do opportunities find us, or do we make our own opportunities? I believe it is a little of both. You should always be looking for them, and then you will find yourself in the right place at the right time.

I grew up on a family farm in Minnesota that has been in the family name since 1879. It was homesteaded by my great-great-grandparents. (My parents still live there.) Back then, this country was growing on the principles that our great nation was founded: opportunities and the belief that you were not held back by anything.

For my great-great-grandparents to make that trip back in 1879, it was a commitment. It was not like you got in a car or plane and you were there in several hours or the next day; it was weeks or months. I can only imagine what they were up against during their trip. It took courage for them to set out on a journey not knowing what they were up against. I'm sure that it took a lot of self-confidence in their abilities and discipline to keep going each and every day. With their destination in mind, they kept their eye on the goal of having a better life or better opportunities.

A couple years after high school, I decided to go into the Army. Just like the generation before me, there were a lot of firsts for me: the first time flying in an airplane, going to a different state that was not touching Minnesota, and the first time being away from family and friends for an extended period of time.

I cannot compare what I did to the journey they endured, but I do understand leaving behind everything you have known to pursue a new opportunity. It takes some guts to step out of your comfort zone and go do something that you want on your own.

But isn't this what makes America different than a lot of the other countries? To have the ability to pursue your dreams for better opportunities for yourself and your family. I think so!

I had the privilege of serving in the Army as a military policeman for almost seven years and got to the rank of staff sergeant. I was stationed on two bases in the United States and one base overseas. Each time I moved, I was welcomed into the new unit. And each time, there were different opportunities for me.

The opportunity I appreciated the most was getting to meet and work with a wide variety of individuals from all the different areas of the United States. What I learned from each and every one of them would change my perception on many things for the rest of my life. For me, it is now one of my "aha" moments in my life and for which I'm so grateful.

I have started to realize that the American Dream, the one thing that we are all looking for, requires the same traits as my great-great-grandparents did back then. It's commitment, courage and self-confidence. With these traits, that dream is within reach. It does not matter where you grew up or what education you had. It does not matter your nationality or the color of your skin. It's your dream. It's your opportunity.

The Army taught me life lessons that were useful after my service. Life after the Army has been good to me, and I owe a lot of it to the Army. When I got out, I went back to school to learn a trade. I have always liked cars, so I went into the auto body field, which led me to opening my own automotive collision repair business. The traits I share with my great-great-grandparents helped me in my business.

The one thing I love about America is that we all have opportunities. I also believe that we are on this earth for one reason and one reason only, and that is to help others!

Once I got out of the Army and finished my technical training, I knew that I wanted to start my own business. The opportunity presented itself just a couple years after school, and boy was I excited! Or should I say "scared." It was the unknowns at the beginning that can cast doubt in your mind. This is what cripples most dreams.

I was now committed to seeing this though at all costs. I have always had a good work ethic, which was mandatory growing up on a farm. The one thing I have always said is that no one will outwork me, and this is another trait to obtaining opportunities and your success.

A business is made up of people, and because of them, my business was successful. There were many individuals who also played a role in my business indirectly that helped me with the areas where I needed assistance. I am grateful for each and every one of them. Because of them, I had the opportunity to sell my business after 25 years.

I love America for all the opportunities it has. I am now looking for my next opportunity.

IT'S YOUR LIFE

It's not a Bon Jovi song; it is the one thing my grandma had always said to me in my adult life.

It's your life, and you have to live it. It is your responsibility, and only you can live it. You know your dreams, what you have always wanted to do, but you don't know where to start. Have the courage to start. You can do this! You just have to take the first step. Then have the discipline to continue on the journey. This will be tough at times, but just keep going.

Be courageous with every opportunity on your journey. You will need a strong commitment, to be self-confident, and have a good work ethic. Your belief in yourself will grow as your dream starts to gain momentum.

Now go out and find your opportunity!

Dominic "Slice" Teich

"Dom "Slice" Teich is a husband, father, Christian, and lover of freedom. He brings his fighter pilot background and applies it to guide pilots, athletes, business owners, and students with afterburner techniques that American fighter pilots use to ensure successful mission completion. As a best-selling author, business owner, entrepreneur, civilian, and military instructor pilot, he knows that busy individuals and teams struggle with information overload.

His blueprint, Single Seat Mindset, is an impactful group of fighter pilot guides who share proven formulas and life advice to peak performers. These techniques and strategies refine and define a purposeful and meaningful life by using proven fighter pilot lessons and tactics. Single Seat Mindset donates all proceeds to a children's cancer non-profit. Visit our life-changing insider-circle today at:

https://SingleSeatMindset.com

Chapter 7

SINGLE-SEAT MEMORIES OF GENERATIONAL CHAOS

Reclined at a 30-degree angle, straps adjusted snugly, radios alive with tactical chatter, visor down with the cueing system on, my wingman in wedge formation, a lukewarm can of my favorite beverage in hand..., there I was, staring at the chaos. With a 36,900 pound, American engineered, single-seat, F-16 jet fighter strapped to my back, I took in the Biblical scenery of the Middle East from 26,000 feet.

Five moves, two deployments, and over thirty world-wide temporary assignments, but this time it was different. I could see the Tigris and Euphrates rivers split in a "Y-shape" northward into Iraq and Syria. Desolate landscape highlighted nomads trekking across the barren desert. The location where Abram originated in Ur was just off the nose of my jet. Abram enabled *generations* of lineage that earned him the ultimate call-sign: "Abraham" the father of a multitude. My fighter pilot call-sign "Slice" paled in comparison.

As the war-ravaged buildings melted to the ground, my thoughts wandered: "Why weren't these countries experiencing the stability, freedom, and wealth of America? Why were the communities, schools, homes, and *institutions* being overrun by terrorist organizations? What was lacking in the institutions that failed to educate each genera-tion? Were American *institutions* creating *genera-tional* chaos?"

Mind + Body + Spirit

Fast forward several years...

"Ravage flight, take it down, set 500 knots."

Advancing the throttle into full military power, I feel the jet firmly press my body back into the seat. The horizon at 5,000 feet fades as the jet slips down to 300 feet above the ground while I look through the clear bubble canopy. Taking in the scenery of the diverse Arizona landscape, I notice fresh water, forests, campgrounds, small towns, eagle nesting sites, radio towers, and civilian airfields... some things to view while ripping by at over 575 miles per hour.

American *institutions* made this possible through teamwork—American teamwork.

Sitting in my single-seat jet fighter, I could think of one thing: **I love America**.

The word "institution" can take on a lifeless, bureaucratic, and manipulative form without context. Those that support institutions may flee when problems arise because of an impersonal connection. Structured Christian institutions with good leadership can ignite purpose, intentionality, and drive. If done in unison, healthy Christian concepts permeate the subconscious minds of the culture, and when put to good use, allow a disciplined, kind, and respectful society that moves in the same direction.

Are the Christian roots that previously created generational stability being twisted from our culture?

Those opposed to non-Christian institutional change have experienced societal pressure when vocalizing good Christian values. Americans spend time on the dynamic aspects of mind and body but largely ignore the life-giving spirituality rooted in Christianity. Without a unified approach to educate the culture about the invisible inner life through virtuous Christian institutions, how does one find the path that generates a daily connection with Christ and lasting happiness?

Freedom For Good

Freedom *from* constraint can lead to freedom *for* comfort. Although more relaxed, in the event of an ejection with no safety constraints in place, a fighter pilot would find ultimate freedom *from* constraint: a free fall towards earth's firm surface. Without the correct Christian fundamentals rooted in our institutions, how does one learn timeless freedom *for* good?

Our forefathers defeated tyranny and allowed us to experience life, liberty, and the pursuit of happiness. Military life, when I joined, allowed classic pro-Christian American ideals defined within the Constitution of the United States. The pursuit of happiness, "becoming free," is a worthwhile cause only if the next generation has a free choice. Freedom and happiness are better served through a framework. Our American culture thrives on a solid foundation of Christianity, which avoids a variable definition of freedom and spirituality. Introducing religious principles allows one to choose, only if institutions within our society allow this information to be shared.

American teamwork led to significant accomplishments. What would happen if human teamwork again highlighted the spiritual needs of humanity?

Our individual freedoms *for* good, and freedom *for* excellence, achieve their lasting nature by holding the individual's <u>will</u> (volition) accountable. A free society is not achievable without a concerted effort to channel each individual within society *for* a more purposeful existence. But why?

Why Should You Care?

Humans become what we love. If we love the material trappings of this world, we will die in a lifeless, material trap; but our souls live on.

It only takes one generation, coupled with institutional decline, to sow the seeds of generational chaos. We aren't lacking answers to historically similar problems. Living during the *Information Age*, one only needs to open a Bible or view current events to see that the world's track record isn't stable. The institutions of our society are failing us. But why?

America's foundations rest upon a Christian judicial system that is based on objective reality rooted in natural law. Through individual enlightenment, man has come to know human nature: body and soul. Living within our nature generates more growth by striving towards good and avoiding evil. Those lives oriented towards good will form virtuous habits. Aligning virtuous habits enables one to act towards the right reason. Right reason, enlightened by faith, brings forth more goodness.

Aristotle offered that happiness is something wholly felt by humans: perfect and complete. Greek moralists concluded we build happy lives through the exercise of virtue, not products of fortune. Learning how to lead a virtuous life starts with academic study but is only *earned* through active *practice*. This completes and perfects human life.

We have a country unlike anywhere else in the world: vast land, physical distance from countries hostile to America, our military, natural resources, diverse human capital, the American Constitution, free enterprise, a country founded on a Christian belief in God, and individual freedoms, to name a few. We will lose the America we know without a unified effort.

Some American institutions are overtly waging war against Christianity. The false freedom of a relativistic worldview, one that has no absolute or universal truth backing what is right or wrong, leads to moral absolutism. This twisted approach is based on popular opinion and not on the common good or natural law. If 51% of the society legalizes murder, is it morally justifiable? Spirituality without a teacher becomes relative. How does one discern truth when there are no truths that are true for everyone? When Americans internalize concepts that aren't rooted in the Constitution and Christian teaching, they risk becoming a slave to the false societal norms that run contrary to the genesis of our great country.

Lasting institutions come alive through a concerted effort put forth by men that are meek but have robust character, and by women that embody traits of feminine genius, such as self-giving, receptivity, maternity, and intuition. So where does one influence change through good institutional leadership, united in Christ's Church, to combat the susceptibility towards the corruption of a fallen humanity?

"Those who cannot see obvious realities are captured by a special type of arrogance—a blind certainty, an imprisonment so total that the prisoner doesn't even know he's locked up."
—D.F. Wallace

How Do We Unite America?

Informed patriotism through self-government is possible. There are reasons to remain hopeful, but hope is only the first step. The strength of America grows from virtuous character traits rooted in each individual citizen. A disciplined effort to grow individually spreads to others by example. A lack of discipline leads to excessive preoccupation with worldly possessions and pleasure that degenerates the culture one person at a time.

Action is contagious; so is lack of action.

In order to experience meaning and purpose, one must be in motion: a change that is toward or away from perfection. Motion generates the feeling of meaning behind the task at hand. As I take to the skies in a single-seat fighter jet, the motion gives meaning to my day. I am doing something. With meaning, I find purpose. With increased purpose, I again add more meaning to my story. The stories of our lives are pieced together one day at a time and require action in order to become meaningful.

American institutions rise to their full potential when individuals are working together for the common good that is rooted in natural law. Individuals within each institution that practice the cardinal virtues of prudence, justice, fortitude, and temperance, and also the theological virtues of faith, hope, and love (charity), create purposeful lives and meaningful societies. The institutional Christian Church creates further growth in the imperfections we cannot gain as individuals.

Our meaningful stories have a cost. This worthwhile cost creates traction and generates movement. Movement coupled with a disciplined effort creates deep stories that lead to connection and a purposeful existence.

FIVE MINUTES A DAY FOR FREEDOM

For those who want to make a positive effect in this world, the question is not about money or material possessions, it's about the time. The thing I know now is that you make time for things that are worthwhile. In fact, you are here now reading this, so I know you have *some time*. It's not how much time you have, it's what you do with the time you have that matters.

The one thing that seems to be universal is that self-discipline is evident in every hero's success story. This magnetic attraction is effective because it is applied every day to an intentional path. To lead a focused life, you'll need a plan, and this is what I suggest. Discipline yourself to invest just *five minutes* at the beginning of each day to sit in silence, meditate, pray, and formulate your plan.

America needs individuals with sound minds, strong characters, and a willingness to make sacrifices to defend our freedoms. Justice allows us to regulate social constructs, but disciplined citizens with virtuous habits create civility and put justice into action.

How many more years do you have?

We will never know, but I bet you have *at least* five minutes.

Jamarrion Tabor

Jamarrion Tabor is a veteran of the United States Navy. She served six years in the Navy as a Yeomen and completed a six-month deployment on two aircraft carriers.

Today, Jamarrion Tabor owns three award-winning, 24-hour childcare centers in the Atlanta metro area.

She is a master when it comes to creating a childcare culture where her employees feel valued, and their contribution to her three locations inspires parents to feel confident that her suite of childcare centers is the right fit for their children. She has mastered employee retention and a wait-list at every center of eager parents who prefer to do business with Jamarrion.

She teaches emerging entrepreneurs how to thrive as profitable multisite childcare owners and operators in the childcare industry.

http://GeorgiasBest24HourChildCare.com

Chapter 8

MAKING A DIFFERENCE THROUGH LOVE

G rowing up on the West Side of Chicago, life was not always easy. My parents had me at the tender age of 16, and throughout my childhood, my mother struggled with drug addiction, which caused me to be raised by my grandmother. I grew up in a low-income area, not the best schools; however, we always had love. I was fortuned to leave my community every day and attend Walt Disney Magnet School. That is when I fell in love with America. For eight hours each day, I was able to leave my community and experience friendships from all areas of Chicago. I was able to experience the melting pot of America and the true culture of our great nation.

Growing up, I decided early that college maybe wasn't for me, but I knew I wanted to travel and see more of America. I wanted to meet people from different cultures and experience the American Dream. My senior year was hectic because I didn't know what I wanted to do. I knew for sure that I didn't want to endure more schooling. However, I was eager to learn about the world.

I had family in the military but never thought it was a place for women. One day after a long day at school, a Navy commercial captured my attention. I was attracted to the diversity and the places that were traveled. I decided to reach out to a recruiter. I was sold on the first conversation. THIS WAS IT! I had to be a part of the Navy.

Bootcamp was not easy; however, it tested my discipline and made me realize what teamwork was all about. I was able to experience different cultures and have conversations with people that I never thought I would meet. After 16 long weeks of bootcamp and Navy A School, I went to Norfolk, Virginia, to start my Navy career.

At 19 years old, I was off to Virginia, and I had never really been outside of Chicago. I was off to see the world and take it all in. I was assigned to the USS Dwight D. Eisenhower; I was in for the surprise of my life because I had no idea how big the ship was. When I arrived, I was scared and excited all in one. I must say, it was a smooth transition, and everyone was very welcoming.

But I was hit with a bombshell; we were set to go on a six-month deployment in four months. Now it gets real. I'd never been away from home, and now I must go overseas for six months! My heart was racing. *"What do I do? How will I survive?"* I told myself, *"Jamarrion, you are from the West Side of Chicago. You can handle anything."* I quickly jumped into survival mode and made a promise to myself that I was going to make the best out of my naval career. I was going to travel to as many places as I could, meet new people and take advantage of what America has to offer.

Over the next 12 months, I visited 10 different countries. I was so intrigued with all the Navy had to offer. My job was a Yeoman; in the civilian world, that would be an administrative assistant. I had the pleasure of serving as the Captain Yeoman. During my time in the Navy, I became a petty officer, and I excelled in the tasks that were placed in front of me, but I still wanted more! After six years in the Navy, I decided that I wanted to still serve; however, I wanted to serve my community. I wanted to go back home and give my community something that it was missing, and that was LOVE! I wanted to find a way to pour into my community and help people understand that anything is possible.

We all talk about the American Dream, and most people think it's a good paying job and a nice home.

For me, it's deeper. It's community, unity, diversity and LOVE. I was determined to give that to my community. I started by holding Women Empowerment Events, going to local shelters and providing "A Day of Beauty" for the residents, which consisted of hair, makeup, nails and motivational speakers. I truly loved that, and I was fulfilled.

With all the crime and hate in the world, I wanted to make a difference, and I wanted to start making a difference with those who are at an early age. I truly believe that love and children are the foundation of our great country. In 2015, I started a home childcare center with the goal to provide quality childcare for low-income children. My goal was to provide a sense of LOVE for the children that were from neighborhoods like the one I grew up in. I wanted to make a difference in the world, and I knew that difference could start from birth.

Since 2015, I have grown my childcare business into three brick-and-mortar locations. My mission is to provide unity and a loving environment, to send children into the world with a loving heart plus morals and values. My hope is to help bring back the unity and love that America is missing by instilling it in our future, which is our CHILDREN. The American Dream is more than a nice paying job and home ownership. It's unity and love, and we can only achieve that by showing love to our neighbors.

SHOW YOUR LOVE

When we learn to operate with love is when our nation can unite. I challenge everyone to show love to your fellow American.

We must take time to really get to know our neighbors. America is a melting pot of LOVE! With unity, we can continue to build a strong nation. I challenge everyone to do something kind every day to pour into our great country.

I challenge my children to not judge and to love thy neighbor because LOVE will always WIN! When you open yourself up to receiving love, it's the same energy as giving it. You're filling your cup and someone else's cup as well.

Candace G. White

Candace White is an active-duty U.S. Marine Corps judge advocate. She has served as a trial counsel, defense counsel, and staff judge advocate in various commands, and currently serves as Appellate Government Counsel.

She has a Masters of Military Law from the Army Judge Advocate General's Legal Center and School and a Masters of Military Studies from the Marine Corps Command and Staff College. Candace is a dedicated triathlete who loves training and competing. Most importantly, Candace is a new mom to Daniel Jackson, with her love, Danny Martinez, U.S. Marine Corps, retired.

Chapter #9

DEFENDING THE CONSTITUTION AND SEEKING EMPATHY

"Empathy is patiently and sincerely seeing the world through the other person's eyes. It is not learned in school; it is cultivated over a lifetime."
—Albert Einstein

My path to joining the Marine Corps was a bit atypical and later in life than most. I graduated law school in 2009 and moved to sunny San Diego to practice law, and in what little free time I expected to have, pursue my passion of racing in triathlons.

I left Chicago, where I grew up, with just two suitcases, my bicycle, and hopes that I had indeed passed the California bar. I moved just days before the results were released so that I would not back down from my plan even if I did not pass. Thankfully (with an exorbitant amount of studying), I survived the 40% pass rate and was sworn into the California bar soon after my arrival in San Diego.

Despite the job market struggles around that time, I was able to secure a job at a small firm, which while not in my ideal area of law, afforded me limited enough billable hours and decent enough pay that I was able to have a pretty good work-life balance filled with lots of swimming, biking, and running.

However, it wasn't long before I realized that this job and lifestyle left me unfulfilled—I sought something more. I wanted a job that wasn't just a 9 to 5, but instead, a calling where I didn't just think but knew I was using the law to make a difference. I had always been drawn to public service, so I began researching job options from various nonprofit organizations to governmental positions.

Like many of my generation, I was deeply impacted by the events of September 11, 2001. I did not grow up in a storied military family but was raised with deep respect and gratitude for our Armed Forces. I had previously thought, when looking at potential colleges, of joining the military, but thought I would have to choose between a career in law and the military.

Then, one day, I cold-called the local San Diego Marine Corps recruitment office. I asked the selection officer if the Marine Corps happened to need any attorneys who also like to compete in triathlons. Long story short, the Marine Corps did, in fact, need such individuals (someone with a law degree who was physically fit and liked to punish, I mean push, themselves). Within a few months, I found myself at the USMC Officer Candidates School in Quantico, Virginia. After ten weeks at OCS, and then another six months at The Basic School, learning to be a provisional rifle platoon commander, I found myself finally, in March of 2012, checking into my first duty station.

My first duty station was Marine Corps Recruit Depot Parris Island, South Carolina, where mostly due to my civilian litigation experience, I was assigned as a trial counsel, which is the Marine Corps equivalent of a prosecutor. I was a 27-year-old second lieutenant, anxious to practice law again. When I first learned my assignment, I was a bit surprised and disappointed. This was the Marine Corps, what kind of "crimes" would I be prosecuting?

I had anticipated and hoped to be doing operational law; I had been anxious to deploy and use my skill sets to support Marine boots on the ground overseas. I had no interest in arguing about parking tickets or other minor infractions in what I imagined would be the bulk of the caseload. I quickly realized my naiveté as to the offenses the Marine Corps, and other Services, regularly litigated amongst its ranks.

Over the next three years and change, my case load would be comprised primarily of cases involving allegations of sexual assault, technology-facilitated crimes against children, and other felony level offenses that I won't get into. Needless to say, it was a stressful and trying time—mentally, physically, and emotionally.

During this tour, I pretty soon became what we colloquially refer to as a "government hack." My work consumed me, and my work was about prosecuting those who committed crimes under the Uniform Code of Military Justice. Granted, the Marines who committed these crimes were in the vast minority. The majority of the Marine Corps is comprised of patriotic, hard-working, generous, fiercely loyal, and law-abiding citizens, and it will forever be my honor and privilege to have served alongside them.

But there is always the, as we say, 10%. The bottom 10% that create 90% of the work. In my case, they created 100% of the work. I worked long hours studying forensic reports, interviewing witnesses and victims, developing case theory and evidence analysis, making sure all my cases were locked up tight to ensure a fair and just conviction. But in doing so, I often had to compartmentalize and even distance myself mentally and emotionally from those involved in the cases. I loved this job and felt I was doing justice for the Marine Corps. So, while it was taxing, it was extremely rewarding.

After completing my tour at Parris Island, I was sent to the Army Judge Advocate General's Legal

Center and School in Charlottesville, Virginia, to earn a master's in military law (LLM). Upon graduation, I was sent overseas to Okinawa where I was told I would be filling a new billet designed to utilize my past litigation experience; I would be the Pacific Regional Complex Defense Counsel. My new job would be to defend Marines who were accused of the types of crimes that just a year ago I had been prosecuting, the Marine Corps equivalent of a public defender.

News of this new role admittedly had me concerned. After all, my over three years of prosecuting had made me a "government hack." How would I handle defending people accused of these crimes? How would I handle the hard conversations that would likely have to be had with my clients? How would I handle interviewing alleged victims from the other side of the table?

I would be lying if I said my next two and half years as a defense counsel were easy. They were not. Those years were some of the most difficult but also most rewarding times of my life. Prior to leaving the United States for Okinawa, my command sent me to an advanced training for public defenders. The training was amazing, and it was inspiring to meet and learn with so many dedicated public defenders who, every day, fight for their clients' rights under the law. At the end of the training, I was asked by someone who was initially very skeptical about my ability to transition from prosecution to public defense, what was one thing I planned to work on going into this new role. My answer was simply, "empathy."

Empathy is simply defined as the ability to identify with or understand another's situation or feelings. I knew that to be an effective and successful defense counsel and do the best job I possibly could for my clients. I had to avoid compartmentalization and not treat them as another case file. I had to develop my ability to empathize with them, if nothing else, as fellow Marines. Regardless of the offenses they were accused of, these were individuals who, like me, had raised their arm and swore an oath to uphold and defend the Constitution. They had said, *"Send me."*

And for an attorney, what better way could I serve my oath to uphold and defend the Constitution than by defending the Constitutional rights of those who had made that same oath; Marines who were at risk of being trampled by the military justice system.

This was very easy to do for clients who I knew were innocent; it was admittedly harder with clients who I knew had committed some often very egregious offenses. But these Marines were more in need of Constitutional protection than possibly any other group I had encountered, and in many cases, I was the only person in their corner. During the next two and a half years, I consistently reminded myself of the experience at training and my personal desire to develop empathy—to be more empathetic to my clients and do my best to understand them, in order to best defend them.

It may seem odd to want to empathize with a suspected criminal. Who would want to put themselves in those shoes and identify with that individual? But these weren't just alleged criminals, they were also Marines. They were fellow Americans who, despite what they may or may not have done related to the case, did serve their country and fellow citizens, often at great sacrifice to self. It was this aspect of humanity that I sought out in each of my clients that I sought to identify with. I sought to find not just some commonality with them but also some common good in them so that I could better empathize with and represent them.

As I said, those years as a defense counsel were some of the most rewarding years of my career and life. I learned an incredible amount about the Marine Corps, the law, and myself. I learned that even those we feel we have nothing in common with, may have traits or histories or beliefs that we can, in fact, relate to, and those connections are worth seeking out. I am forever grateful that I had the opportunity to serve those Marines and the Marine Corps in that role.

As I have moved to other duty stations and served in other billets, I have continued my pursuit of empathy. I have also encouraged others to seek empathy. Find the commonalities you may have with another person. Understand the differences. Embrace what unifies you, such as service to your country, and seek to create more unification than division.

This applies not just to the military but also to American society today. With the growth of social media, we are more connected than ever, but we are less engaged on a personal level. Fewer conversations take place in person, replaced by interactions through cold, impersonal screens and in 140 characters or less. While the growth of connectivity is a wonderful thing, we as a society need to be mindful that there is no replacement for human-to-human connections, in person, with open dialogue, and a willingness to not just be heard but also to listen and seek to understand. That is how you learn about others and grow personally. That is how you can develop empathy. Empathy that can, in turn, lead to incredible relationships as you realize you have more in common with people than you previously realized.

So have those discussions. Be open. Be honest. Seek to understand commonalities and differences. In other words, seek empathy in your own life. You may be amazed at not just how many relationships you develop but also how much you learn about yourself.

It was through an active pursuit of <u>empathy</u> that I turned from a "government hack" to what many in my field would call a "defense hack." I am extremely proud of this label as it came from fulfilling my oath to the Constitution in what I consider the purest form: defending the rights of those who defend our rights. I encourage you, regardless of your profession, beliefs, or upbringing, to also seek <u>empathy</u>.

"There is no limit to the amount of good you can do if you don't care who gets the credit."

—President Ronald Reagan

THERE IS NO LIMIT TO THE AMOUNT OF GOOD YOU CAN DO

President Reagan has some of my favorite quotable quotes, and this one is no exception. Many jobs and roles, whether it be a Service member, a grocer, a stay-at-home mother, or many others, often are underappreciated and don't get the credit they deserve. But these roles, and the work they do, are indispensable for society and are often most effective because they do what they do for the good of others and not for the credit.

Society is often focused on and even driven by, getting credit. People want more likes on their social media posts or a bigger bonus for contributions at work. But when you stop focusing on the credit, and more on the impact of your efforts, there truly is no limit to the amount of good you can do and the lives you can positively impact. So, my recommendation is stop caring as much about the likes, the money, and the credit, but instead, try to focus more on the good you can do and are doing, the goals you accomplish, the lives you touch, and the people you inspire.

It will be worth it.

Kevin Stokes

Kevin Stokes is an Idaho native who spent nearly 13 years in the Idaho Army national Guard. He has 1,500 hours, with 480 hours in combat, as an AH-64A Apache helicopter pilot.

He was qualified as a dual-seat instructor pilot, maintenance test pilot and served as his battalion's aviation safety officer. He and his wife, Susan, (when she's not homeschooling their four children) run a real estate and note investing company.

Kevin believes that investing in yourself makes you a better person, which in turn, makes for a stronger family. Strong families build better communities. This is the only way to ensure there will be liberty for generations to come. Kevin knows that anyone, with the right teacher, can successfully invest. You can get your note investing action guide right now by visiting:

https://BlueHorizonNotes.com/take-action

Chapter #10

TAKE ACTION
WHEN OTHERS WON'T

A merica is the greatest nation on Earth. It has amazing landscapes, from rugged mountain ranges and fertile plains to near endless coastlines. All of these features set the stage for America to be a land of abundance and opportunity.

The roots of Western civilization are centuries old, but America's beauty comes from its embrace of liberty. Freedom is the ability to do as you choose, but liberty exists when freedom is combined with morality. Our founders didn't make this up out of thin air; they pulled it from their English history.

In 1014 AD, the English King Aethelred made a pact with his subjects to place limits on government over the people. The Charter of Liberties, in 1100, addressed the abuses of royal power. The Magna Carta, in 1215, attempted to restrain King John in order to make peace with rebellious barons. In 1689, the English Bill of Rights forced the Crown to seek the consent of the people through Parliament. These great documents clearly serve as the basis of the U.S. Constitution. For over one thousand years, English and American governments have individual liberty.

In reading the Amendments, you will find "life, liberty, or property." But they are not listed as ideas. All three are possessions, and possessions must be cherished and defended through moral action. The key to defense is taking action.

It is astounding to note that the founding of our government is centered squarely on what it needed to ensure human flourishing.

But human flourishing is only possible when people take action.

"There are risks and costs to action.
But they are far less than the long-range risks of
comfortable inaction."
—John F. Kennedy

Liberty has created an environment where millions of people from every continent have left all they had or knew to come to America. Our history is filled with such action-takers because only in America could they have liberty. My own family has immigrants only three generations back.

When I joined, I learned the U.S. Army is really good at teaching people how to do things by the book. I'm positive that somewhere my basic training drill sergeant still has a training manual containing the tasks, conditions, and standards required for emptying his trash can.

I attended the Warrant Officer Candidate Course (WOC) prior to starting the Army's helicopter flight training at Fort Rucker, Alabama. The WOC Course is where folks with even a touch of obsessive-compulsive disorder are celebrated and rewarded. Everything in life during the course, including folding your underwear and how you put your spoon down during mealtime, was documented in painstaking detail. All of which, you were held accountable for. The rigid nature of these schools influenced me a great deal, and I fell into getting permission before I did anything. It didn't stop me from acting, but it did slow me down, if for no other reason than to avoid confrontation.

It wasn't until I met my friend, Chief Warrant Officer 4 Andy Isaac, before I understood I should not wait for others' permission to do anything.

He and I were in the same unit in the Idaho Army national Guard, and we were activated in 2006 for a deployment to Afghanistan. Andy and I were both AH-64A Apache pilots, but we were of vastly different experience levels.

Andy began his flying career as a Huey helicopter crew chief in Vietnam. Later, he used his GI Bill to earn his private pilot's license on his way to earning multiple commercial and instrument ratings in both fixed wing and rotary wing aircraft.

During one of our earliest missions together, I asked Andy how many flight hours he had.

I will never forget his response, *"I quit counting when I crossed 28,000."*

This was astonishing because I had just completed 300 hours. I followed up, *"When was that?"*

"Probably five or six years ago."

It was stunning to think this man probably had more time in an aircraft with his eyes shut due to blinking than I had in my entire career. We would fly over 150 combat hours together. He taught me many lessons, but the most important was not about flying at all.

Six months into our deployment, our unit took part in a large mission out of Jalalabad. We were tasked with flying security for Blackhawks and Chinooks that moved troops or ran resupply missions all over the region. At the time, there were over 2,000 Army Infantry and Marines scattered throughout northeastern Afghanistan.

That terrain is perhaps the most rugged on Earth, and it doesn't take long to grind men and equipment into dust.

As that operation wound down, the utility helicopters began redeploying troops from places like the Korengal valley back to Jalalabad. As an aircrew, Andy and I were tasked with flying security for these flights. By the end of each day, there were exhausted troops everywhere on the airfield awaiting further transport back to Bagram. These men were haggard, and some of them had uniforms so shredded they looked like cargo shorts. Jalalabad supply said there weren't any replacement uniforms for them.

Jalalabad had an area filled with dozens of 40-foot shipping containers that every aircraft would fly past. We were on approach for landing on our last escort flight when Andy asked me, *"How long have we been here at Jalalabad?"*

"This rotation has been 3 weeks and 4 days," I replied, *"But who's counting?"*

"That's what I thought." After a short pause, he continued, *"In that time, have you seen anyone open those containers?"*

"No, why?"

"When these ground pounders are all gone, you and I are going shopping."

A couple of weeks later, he and I were standing in front of one of the shipping containers. It was obviously locked and sealed. The printed manifest on one of the doors was faded, but we could see the date of arrival was the year before.

We checked a few more, and they were the same.

Secured but forgotten.

We opened one at random, and inside from top to bottom, front to back was nothing but beautiful two by six boards. The next container was filled with ¾ inch plywood sheets. The third container was filled with cardboard boxes of brand-new Army uniforms. Andy said something about the Infantry guys being pissed if they knew that they were minutes away from brand-new uniforms.

Back on the flight line, our maintainers operated out of a couple of shipping containers. One served as a small office, the other held supplies. For the next few weeks, whenever we weren't flying, Andy and I, along with the rest of the unit, put the lumber to good use.

We built a shaded area between the containers. The shade became a popular place, and people started hanging out when off duty.

The flight line was just gravel in those days, so we built a deck in front of the office container door. There was not enough shade, so the deck got a roof. And since the roof looked like a half-finished Old West store, we built a sign to complete the look. Andy came up with the name.

"Shit Creek Paddle Company. Established 2006" in 24-inch letters so as to be read from the runway. It wasn't uncommon to see transient aircraft stop to take a picture.

Suffice it to say, Jalalabad operations' leadership were not very pleased. In short order, Andy and I were rotated out to another base, and we never spent another night at Jalalabad. To this day, I'm not sure that wasn't Andy's plan the whole time.

I think of that year in Afghanistan quite often and Jalalabad in particular. We took a miserable situation and made it better in small ways. It was there that I learned that asking for forgiveness is better than asking for permission. In most cases, forgiveness isn't necessary.

In spite of the last couple of years, I believe America's greatest days are in front of it. We have reached a tipping point in history where technology has quietly expanded liberty. People inside and outside of America are starting to see that liberty is theirs to take, and they don't have to ask anyone for it.

Andy Isaac and Kevin...

... and their handiwork.

DON'T COMPLAIN.
DO SOMETHING.

"The number one responsibility for each of us is to change ourselves with hope that others will follow."
— Ron Paul

Most humans appear subdued and unfocused. It seems they live for nothing more than to be entertained and pacified. But if you look at it from a different perspective, most people are uninspired by their surroundings, and they know not what to do. This leaves them waiting for others to lead the way.

You can lead the way. It is simple, but it won't be easy; things worth doing seldom are. Prepare yourself to do hard things.

Get in shape. Learn a new skill. Better still, teach one to someone else. Write a book. Start a business. Seek a new job.

Imagine if you doubled or tripled or 10x your income. Would others notice? I doubt they would notice, but you sure would. Others will notice your actions, and they will be inspired.

This is what America needs, and more importantly, so do you.

John Klesaris

John Klesaris is a U.S. Army veteran of the Military Intelligence Corps, with training and experience as a Korean linguist and translator. The study to achieve proficiency in a <u>very</u> foreign language taught him that intense focus and commitment helps anyone overcome tough challenges in both life and business. He brings a "can-do" attitude to tasks, drawing heavily on his military background and building on that through his work as a business consultant and coach.

While stationed in South Korea, he gained invaluable insight into the human condition by working with and living among people of a very different culture. John cherishes the time he spent with the Korean people, continuing to reflect on lessons learned there. He entered the military from a job as a licensed plumber, and he launched into business within a year of leaving the military, being self-employed for over 25 years.

Chapter 11

DO IT!

Americans today are under a barrage of challeng-es, both personal and professional. People are questioning long-established norms with fervor, confusing everyday hard-working people. Some even suggest that our country and her offer of freedom are on the wane and will soon fade into history.

Nonsense!

I'm here to tell you that the American Dream is alive and well and that true patriots smart enough to pick up this book will never surrender the values that America stands for. The ideals that sparked the revolution in 1776 and saved Europe from itself in World War II. The ideals that bring tens of thousands of American volunteers from all walks of life to defend freedom all over the world. It was the love for those same ideals that inspired me to join the military, from a very young age.

In fact, here's a funny story. While attending school one day, I saw a postcard for the Marine Corps. It was an information request that you filled out and mailed, which would then likely be forwarded to a local recruiter. Mesmerized by the crisp uniform on the Marine in the advertisement, I filled it out and dropped it in the mailbox before leaving school.

In about a week, I received a letter from a Marine Corps Major, signed in real ink. It read:

> Dear John,
>
> I am excited to hear about your interest in the Marine Corps. Today's military offers excellent opportunities for young men willing to commit to our country's defense, as well as assistance for college tuition and generous benefits.
>
> However, since you are only twelve, it will be some time before you can become a Marine...

It went on to say that the Marine Corps wanted me to stay in school and that he wanted me to inquire again when I was older. Now, I knew I was too young to enlist at that point, but it didn't stop me from starting the process to see what would happen. It's part of the <u>DO IT</u> mentality.

Inspiration

Experience has shown me that people who enlist in the military do so in part because they have at least some appreciation for the American experiment and the ideals that it inspired. In my case, I discovered my love for the ideals of freedom and opportunity at a very young age. I was always interested in the Founding Fathers, the struggles they faced and the events that led to the Revolutionary War. In fact, I can't remember a time when I wasn't intrigued by those things.

When I was a young boy, one of my older brothers showed me a commemorative stone (we called it the "Hancock Rock") in the deep woods behind our home. It's in a place you would never find unless someone showed it to you. It marks the Amos Wyman Homestead, a place where John Hancock and Sam Adams hid from the British on a tense night in 1775.

For years after, and even to this day, I visit whenever I face a personal challenge and think about Hancock and Adams standing in that very spot wondering what their next move would be. Remember, the first shots of the Revolutionary War in nearby Lexington had not yet been fired, but Hancock and Adams were already hunted men, wanted for treason against the Crown. It didn't stop them though; they decided to <u>DO IT</u> (plan the revolution).

It doesn't matter when one discovers how great our country is. For some, it's acquired later in life. But once it happens, that appreciation is not easily given up.

Enlistment

When I enlisted in the Army, I had already earned a master plumber's license in Massachusetts. The recruiters told me that I could attain advanced rank in a year and have my own crew if I chose that career track in the military. Instead, I chose the linguist program in military intelligence, not because I didn't want to do plumbing (or get advanced promotion), but because I wanted to maximize my learning experience.

Struggle

After basic training, I was stationed at the Defense Language Institute in Monterey, California, one of the most beautiful duty stations in the world. I was assigned to the 47-week course in Korean, to my initial dismay. Being of Greek descent, I wanted Russian, since they bear similarities, and it was a European-based language rooted in Greek. Korean

was a whole different ball game, having no associa-
tion with English whatsoever. It was also considered
a "Category Four" language (on a difficulty level of
one to four), and I would likely be sent to Korea after
training. This is a hardship tour, meaning family and
belongings can't officially go with you.

All things considered, I was envious of my col-
leagues assigned to easier languages, like Spanish
(Category One, with stations in Key West, Florida) or
Russian (Category Three, with stations in Europe). I
wondered about luck. Regardless, the Army doesn't
care about your feelings; they just put you where you
are needed. So, with some grit and the DO IT mentality, I embraced the learning process. And what a
process it was! Reading, writing, listening, and
speaking for seven hours every working day. Intense
study, three to four hours each night, trying to keep
up with the insane learning pace.

After 47 weeks, I passed the language tests and
moved on to the specialized training associated with
this skill set, which was equally challenging. There
were many times when I feared I would not make the
grade.

I was later stationed in South Korea, near a place
at the demilitarized zone that few have seen up close.
It's a step back in time because not much has
changed there since the cease-fire from 1953, which
brought the Korean war to a halt. It is deeply hum-

bling to be a mere stone's throw from a place where freedom is unknown to most and open hostility permeates the air. Ironically, many of our North Korean brethren can only dream about freedom whether through words, deeds. or even thoughts.

Our unit provided tactical electronic warfare support to the Second Infantry Division, remaining in a constant state of readiness due to the unpredictable nature of North Korea. Alerts and drills were common, and we were never certain whether it was practice or the real thing. To say it is a tense part of the world is an understatement.

Rewards

I enjoyed my work, in particular the soldiering part of it. I had the distinct privilege of serving under Captain Paul Nakasone (now General Nakasone, U.S. Cyber Command and Director, national Security Agency), who is a true soldier and military leader in every sense of the word. He instilled a deep appreciation for the tactical nature of our mission, despite all the high-tech equipment the Army employs in modern warfare. At its core, our Army is still a ground-pounding fighting force that encounters hand-to-hand combat as part of the mission.

It was then that I earned early promotion to the NCO Corps, ahead of my college-educated peers who had outranked me since our early days at the language school because they had degrees. It reminded me that certificates hanging on the wall don't ensure success and that hard work is still recognized (and rewarded) by watchful eyes.

I returned stateside with first-hand insight into the plight of the industrious Korean people who have endured hardships in that region for hundreds of years. At a deeper level, I gained a fresh appreciation for America's place in the world and our struggle against communism, dictators, and tyrants and why these struggles abroad are important for us at home.

These four years in the military have had a profound impact on my thought processes and approaches to all things in life. They inspire me when I'm excited, reminding me of the DO IT mentality whenever I'm challenged. I firmly believe that it is this attitude that dominated my parents' generation during World War II, and it is my hope that it will inspire modern Americans both young and old in the same way. By serving a purpose greater than ourselves, we receive rewards that are more profound than anything someone can "give" us.

Results

Within a year of leaving the Army, I bought my first home and opened a plumbing business. In less than two years, I bought a second home and two years later added a consulting business. Since then, I've trained and coached hundreds of entrepreneurs all over America in business marketing, management, financial statements and employee training, both individually and in workshop environments. I conduct similar training to business associations, helping thousands grow membership and instill business training to their members.

Taking action has made all the difference for me, opening doors I never thought could be opened.

While I've incorporated many military practices into my work, none have helped me more than pushing beyond what is believed possible, what I call the <u>DO IT</u> mentality.

Put it to work for you and for America!

LIGHT A FIRE!

"Freedom is never more than one generation away from extinction. We didn't pass it to our children in the bloodstream. It must be fought for, protected, and handed on for them to do the same, or one day we will spend our sunset years telling our children and our children's children what it was once like in the United States where men were free."

– Ronald Reagan

Your decision to take action will lift others to new heights, either by inspiration or by direct involvement. Your focused (even <u>stubborn</u>) persistence creates waves of change for you and those around you. Grab the bull by the horns and embrace the challenge that's scaring you the most. Show everyone what you're capable of. This <u>DO IT</u> mentality built American strength AND her beacon of freedom, and it will continue building it for decades more. Your success breeds success in others, preserving the gift of freedom we've been given.

There are more opportunities for success than at any other time in our history. Don't be fooled into thinking otherwise; just be the American that you were born to be!

"IRON" Mike Steadman

"IRON" Mike Steadman is a United States Naval Academy graduate, Marine Corps Infantry officer, and Hoover Veteran Fellow at Stanford University's Hoover Institution. He's the author of the book, *Black Veteran Entrepreneur: Validate Your Business Model, Build Your Brand, and Step into Your Greatness.*

After leaving active duty in 2015, following deployments to Afghanistan, Japan, and the Philippines, Mike relocated to Newark, NJ, where he went on to found IRONBOUND Boxing, a nonprofit that provides free amateur boxing training, entrepreneur education, and employment opportunities for Newark youth and young adults. Mike and his partner, Keith Colon, oversee the legendary IRONBOUND Boxing Academy.

A few years later, he founded IRONBOUND Media, a brand strategy firm serving veteran-owned small business owners.

https://IRONBOUNDMedia.com

Chapter 12

MOTHER TO SON: THE GIFT OF THE AMERICAN DREAM

For some people, it's never been easier than now to look pessimistically towards the American Dream, the belief that in the land of opportunity, everyone can create their own version of success, be it financial or otherwise.

It seems like every time we cut on the news or check our social media feeds nowadays, we're constantly being bombarded with hate, discontent, and all the negative things wrong with America instead of what makes us truly special. At our core, we are a melting pot of all races, ethnicities, and genders, with opportunities to achieve economic and social mobility, regardless of who you are or where you come from.

Don't get me wrong, over the last few years, we've been through a lot as a nation, including a global pandemic due to COVID-19, racial unrest in the aftermath of the death of George Floyd, and what feels like a never-ending political divide, fueled by a 24/7 news cycle. By no means are we perfect, and we still have a long way to go, but the American Dream still exists for those willing to sacrifice and put in the necessary work to define it and achieve it for themselves.

Growing up, I didn't always believe this, even though my mother, Willeen Steadman, a high school educator and special education director, did her best to reinforce this belief in me. I was young, naive, and had to witness it for myself before I could become a true believer.

My first indication that she was right was upon receiving an official appointment to attend the United States Naval Academy in Annapolis, Maryland.

A few years prior, attending the Naval Academy felt like a long shot for a young black kid from East Texas with subpar grades, low test scores, and little to no physical prowess. None of which mattered to my mother who raised my older sister, Candace, and me by herself while working multiple jobs to keep food on the table and make sure we were provided for.

From the moment I expressed interest in attending Annapolis to my mother, she did everything in her power to put me in position to get in, including hiring a tutor, driving me to various networking events, and even working with me on my application essays. Through her love, support, and belief in me, my own confidence grew.

"My son is going to Annapolis, just you watch," she said to every skeptic she came across, including a local Army veteran who thought I didn't have a chance in hell.

Till this day, I remember sitting across from him at his office on the campus of Texas A&M University, just a few miles from where we lived in Bryan-College Station, as he looked me dead in my eyes and told me Annapolis was a pipe dream. Maybe for him, but not for us.

It wasn't easy, and there were no guarantees the entire time, but after six SAT's, countless hours of tutoring, and a lot of sacrifice, I was given the opportunity to attend the Naval Academy Preparatory School in Newport, Rhode Island, for a year, where I earned the necessary grades to receive an official appointment to the Academy the following year.

Not only did I go on to attend Annapolis and graduate, but I also became a 3x collegiate boxing champion, as a member of the U.S. Naval Academy Boxing Team, and earned a commission as a Marine officer, along the way.

I'll never forget the feeling of accomplishment I felt having my mother there with me to celebrate on graduation day from the Naval Academy. Despite her suffering from a hemorrhagic stroke during my sophomore year, which left her permanently paralyzed, she already did her part helping me get in, and she went on to pin my lieutenant bars on my collar, signifying my status as a commissioned officer.

After graduation, I spent the next five years as a Marine Infantry officer, deploying to Afghanistan, Japan, and the Philippines, with 1st Battalion 8th Marines, out of Marine Corps Base Camp Lejeune in NC. The opportunity to serve as an Infantry officer felt like I was a first-round draft pick in the national Football League. Leading a platoon of Infantry Marines was one of the most sought-after positions in the entire Marine Corps, and yet here I was. The Marines built my confidence as a leader while also cultivating my passion for service, in uniform and out. During my five years, I did everything I set out to do, including becoming an Infantry officer, leading a platoon in combat, and earning the respect of my Marines and fellow officers.

Although I enjoyed my time in the Marines, I had other plans after the service, including using the leadership skills that I developed, to serve youth and young adults in inner-city America. Boxing was good to me at the Naval Academy and served as an anchor to help me deal with my mom's stroke. It also exposed me to the plight of other young black men and women in the inner-city while training at boxing gyms in places like Southeast D.C., Baltimore, and New York City. Through these experiences, I developed an affinity for young people in the inner-city who grew up in single-parent homes like me, but without a strong support network.

I relocated to Newark, New Jersey, in 2015, where I went on to establish the IRONBOUND Boxing Academy, a free boxing gym for Newark youth and young adults, with the mission of building champions "in and out of the ring." Virtually overnight, I officially became an entrepreneur, which is something I never thought possible during my younger days.

Why Newark?

While at the Naval Academy, I spent two summers teaching leadership at St. Benedict's Preparatory School in Newark, New Jersey, a private school that caters to young men and women of color. As a result, Newark felt like the perfect place to build my gym.

Today, I look at the world I've built for myself and sit in awe. Not only do I run a nonprofit, but I'm also a published author, speaker, and business coach. None of this would have been possible if it wasn't for my mother cultivating the American Dream within me. She saw my potential from the very beginning. Although there's been a lot of pain and heartache along the way, when I look at myself in the mirror, considering where I came from, it's impossible for me to deny the existence of the American Dream.

My life isn't perfect, and by no means am I printing money, but I've done amazing things and been to amazing places that my younger self thought were off -limits for me. Even as I write this, I'm sitting in a conference room at Stanford University's Hoover Institution, where I'm a member of the inaugural class of the Hoover Veteran Fellows, a year-long fellowship for a select group of military veterans to address real-world challenges through impact-driven projects, under the resources and tutelage of the Hoover Institution.

Don't let today's negativity distract you from the opportunity to achieve the American Dream. It's waiting for you. Now go out and achieve it. When you do, write me. I look forward to reading about your journey.

EMBRACE THE STOCKDALE PARADOX

"You must maintain unwavering faith that you can and will prevail in the end, regardless of the difficulties, and at the same time, have the discipline to confront the most brutal facts of your current reality, whatever they might be."
– James B. Stockdale

Whenever life gets hard, remember the Stockdale Paradox above. Admiral Stockdale was a United States Naval Academy graduate and Hoover Institution Fellow, who spent over seven years as a prisoner of war during the Vietnam War, in the infamous "Hanoi Hilton" prison camp. Despite the hardships and constant uncertainty of whether or not he and others would return home again, Stockdale accepted the most brutal facts of his current reality but never lost faith he would get home.

Life is hard at times for everyone whether you're running a business, dealing with the death of a loved one, or searching for meaning and purpose in your own life. Don't be afraid to confront the brutal facts, whatever they are, but have faith that things will work out in the end.

Gary T. Dyer

Gary T. Dyer is a sales professional that served in the United States Marine Corps for 12 years. During his tour on active duty, Gary primarily served as an aviation mechanic for both the CH-46 helicopter and the V-22 Osprey tiltrotor aircraft. Along his journey, Gary was awarded for several meritorious achievements in the superior performance of duties while serving as a V-22 Osprey mechanic instructor, instructor evaluator, master training specialist, and course scheduler for the Center for Naval Aviation Technical Training.

Today, with 15 years of experience in the private sector, working with numerous industries and in various high-level capacities, he has successfully helped many of them in generating multi-millions of dollars of revenue through leadership, management, business process improvement, automation, sales, and marketing. If you would like to increase your sales and see if Gary can help you, visit:

https://GaryTDyer.com

Chapter #13

GIVING BACK: THE SECRET TO LIVING AND ACHIEVING THE AMERICAN DREAM

In today's fast-paced society, millions of people are chasing their vision of the American Dream. For some, that dream means having a huge mansion and a fast car, such as a Lamborghini, sitting in their driveway. For others, like me, their version of the American Dream is having enough money to meet their needs, a close relationship with their family, and a safe environment to raise their kids. That is one of the many things that makes America the greatest nation in the world. Each of us has the freedom to choose what our American Dream truly means to us. For me, I have found my secret to achieving and living my American Dream. My secret is quite simple and can be expressed in two words: _Giving Back_. Let me explain and share a bit of my journey in finding this secret.

You see, I believe in the true American spirit of people who are ambitious, giving, and are passionate to make their dreams come true. As a child growing up in a rural family in Kentucky, I have learned from some of the greatest role models on this planet that if you work hard, are ambitious, giving of your time, and passionate about your dreams, then anything can come true. These role models were not some big movie stars nor public figures. They were my father, mother, grandmothers, grandfathers, uncles, aunts, and coaches in youth sports.

None of them ever gave up on their dreams nor blamed their environment or circumstances during my childhood. Overall, these role models in my life and the values that I have learned from them are what shapes me into who I am today. The one ideal they taught me that stands out is _Giving Back_.

During my childhood, there were countless occasions in which I learned firsthand about the secret of _Giving Back_. For example, I can recall when I was about 10 years old and in the dead of winter when my mother taught me the importance of _Giving Back_. You see, I grew up in an area that had a few neighbors that lived close by, and as a little boy, I was always running around playing tag, having snowball fights with my brothers or building snowmen during the winter months. Just being a kid. One evening, I was heading home from playing with a friend down the road, and I cut through a neighbor's backyard. Around the back of the property was a very small, silver mobile home that was in very rough condition. My brothers and I had always been told that no one lived there and that it was haunted. (You know how kids can tell some far-fetched stories.)

Well, as I came upon the old, run-down silver trailer, I was stopped dead in my tracks by what I saw. There in front of the door to the trailer was an old man facedown in the snow! The front door to the trailer was wide open, and the old man wasn't moving or making a sound. Needless to say, I was scared to death. Instantly, a million thoughts went through my mind. *"Was he dead? Is he hurt?"* I didn't know what to think! What would you have done as a 10-year-old kid in that situation? Well, I did the first thing that came to my mind; I ran to my mother to tell her what I just saw.

As I reached my house and burst the door open so hard it nearly came off the hinges, I yelled, *"Mom, Mom, there's an old man facedown in the snow at the old silver trailer!!! We have to help him!"*

My mother very calmly grabbed her coat and gloves and said, *"Calm down, calm down...let's go help him."*

As we walked around to the front door of the old silver trailer, I was shaking beyond belief and extremely scared. Here was this old man, lying facedown in the snow, and the temperature was at least in the mid-twenties. As we approached the old man, my mother asked, "*Sir, are you alright?*"

After my mother asked a few more times, the old man yelled out, "*Please help me!*"

Thank goodness! He was alive! As my mother, very calmly, began to tell me to get on the other side of him, she told me to help lift him up. After some lifting and slipping around in the snow, we were able to get the gentleman onto his feet. After a few minutes, my mother and I helped him get back into his home and sit him down at his little table. It was at this point that I was about to learn what the true meaning of <u>*Giving Back*</u> was all about.

Once we (really my mother) had helped the gentleman calm down from this traumatic event, she began to ask him if he was hurt, if he wanted her to call any family, or needed to go to the hospital. After a few seconds, the old man just looked up at her and said, "*Ma'am, I'm OK. I can't thank you and your boy enough for saving my life. I would have frozen to death if you hadn't helped me.*" My mother told him that no thanks were needed and that we were just glad that we could help.

I can remember at that time I asked, "*Sir, do you want my mom to call some of your family and let them know that you are OK?*"

I can recall like it was yesterday what the old man said next. He said with tears streaming down his worn face, "*Son, I don't have anyone for your mom to call. I don't have any family left.*"

I didn't know what to say! I felt so sad at that moment that I began to tear up. It was at that moment that my mother said "*Sir, that's alright. You have us as your family right now. We're going to take care of you.*"

I remember looking up at my mother with pure joy in my heart and saying, "*Thanks, Mom.*" I was so proud of my mother. I could just feel the love and compassion that shined through in that moment to help this gentleman. It just gave me chills that we were helping him. At this point, my mother and I went back home, and she proceeded to fix him the biggest plate of food that you have ever seen. As a good ole country Kentucky Mom, she knew how to cook. After everything was ready, we took the food over to the old man and stayed with him as he devoured more than half of the plate. I can still remember that big smile on his face after eating.

When it was time to go that night, we made sure he was all safe and sound in his home before we left. We said goodnight and walked back to our house. Once we got inside, my mother sat down with me at our kitchen table and said, "*You know you did a good thing today, and I'm very proud of you.*" She continued to say, *"Always remember that no matter how much or how little you have to offer someone, it's always important to give what you can and help people in need. If you do that, you'll live a good life."*

Looking back now, all these years later, there it was—the secret to achieving the American Dream—*Giving Back!* I will always love you for that wisdom, Mom! Just in case you were wondering, my mother and I continued to help that gentleman for several months after that evening before he passed away. I'll never forget that time for as long as I live.

Throughout the rest of my life to this point, I took those life lessons and applied them whether I thought about it at the time or not. During my service as a U.S. Marine, I applied the secret of *Giving Back* in a few different ways as well. I volunteered to be a mentor for every Special Olympics that I could attend as well as volunteered, with my sons, for many Thanksgiving events at our local United Service Organization at Camp Lejeune.

After my service to our GREAT nation, I have also spent several years helping to give back by coaching youth football. As you can see, I have taken those early life lessons and the secret of *Giving Back* to enrich my life to achieve and live MY version of the American Dream. I hope this chapter inspires each of you to achieve and live your American Dream as well!

"GIVE BACK"

Those two simple words can be used to keep our society, our culture, and our GREAT nation strong for many centuries to come if you're willing to apply them in your daily life. The question is: What are you willing to *Give Back?*"

That's what makes me so proud to be an American and a veteran! We have the freedom to choose what we want to give back. For some, that might be in the form of money. For others, it might be in the form of time, such as volunteering. If each of us are willing to "Give Back" in whatever form that means to you, America will always be the land of the free and the home of the brave! Here are just some ways to Give Back:

- Donate your old clothes to your community Goodwill, church, or school.
- Volunteer at a local food bank or homeless shelter.
- Sign up to be a mentor in a local youth program.
- Offer to help with youth groups or sporting events at your local schools.

PART 3

WHAT NEXT?

"Americans never quit."

—General Douglas MacArthur

AMERICAN ENDS IN
"I CAN"

When I was about five or six, I remember seeing a red, white and blue round pin, the kind worn in the old days during elections, that proudly proclaimed:

AMERICAN
ENDS IN
I CAN!

Fast forward 50 years and I still remember reading that like it was yesterday and the profound effect it had on me when I realized the simple truth behind those five words.

As I mentioned in the beginning of this book, my sole reason for publishing this book and book series is to share the wisdom, ideas, experiences, and challenges from everyday folks who all want to see our country remain the beacon of liberty and opportunity she has been for all who call her home and those who seek to call her home in the future.

I would not be telling the truth if I did not say there are days (even during this book project) where I wonder if things are beyond the point of hope. And then something happens to remind and encourage me that we can affect change, that we can do good for the collective whole, and that traditional American values are still definitely worth fighting for.

My hope is that each person reading these very words has been energized in some small (or big) way, and more importantly, now has an idea on something they can do to make America stronger. When I shared this vision with Tracey Brown (Chapter #3) during a call I had with her, she said, "*Mike, all big waves start out as little ripples.*"

I immediately wrote it down when she said it and now use it to encourage you to create a little ripple. Maybe it is just within your family. Maybe it is within your school district. Maybe within your local community. Or maybe there is an even bigger opportunity in front of you.

Regardless, I want to remind you, YOU CAN! And when life and daily events, and pessimistic people get in the way, I want you to say to yourself, "*I CAN!*"

—**Mike Capuzzi**

ABOUT
I LOVE AMERICA BOOKS

The book you are currently reading is the first book in what we hope will be a long series of inspirational and helpful books *by the people, for the people.*

Each edition will include a distinct and focused group of 13 contributing authors who have a deep love for America and want to see her get stronger and healthier. This book (and all future books in the series) has three primary goals:

1. To provide a series of themed short books that are quick and easy to read and share practical and actionable advice all Americans can use.

2. To provide a unique platform for "everyday" Americans to share their love, stories, hope, and ideas for America via a published book.

3. To support worthwhile and valuable causes. Each book will support a specific nonprofit organization. For every book sold, we will donate $1.00 to that organization for the entire first year of publication.

Potential Future Book Ideas

There are several future book ideas in the works, including specific editions that feature:

- Business owners
- Health and wellness professionals
- Young entrepreneurs
- Students (high school, college, tech)
- Law enforcement professionals
- Teachers
- Moms
- Dads
- Grandparents
- And more!

If you would like to be considered for the opportunity of being a contributing author in a future edition, please let us know!

Fill out the Contributing Author Information Invitation by visiting:

https://ILoveAmericaBooks.com

CONTRIBUTING AUTHOR INTERVIEW DIRECTORY

Each of the following contributing authors are available for podcast, radio, TV, article, and other media interviews. Feel free to contact them.

Paul White, whitehouseops@gmail.com
Winning, discipline, character, planning

Andrew Hibbard, connect@andrew-hibbard.com
Medicare marketing, lead generation, sales strategies

Tracey Brown, https://linktr.ee/TBConsulting
Mindset, excellence, fun/getting unstuck

Jeff Arnold, interviewjeff@jeffarnold.com
Business, leadership, buying companies, insurance

CONTRIBUTING AUTHOR DIRECTORY

Brandi Barnard "BB" King, bbking4freedom.com
Motherhood, aviation, liberty, strength in Christ

Jody Gatchell, jody@beawesome2.com
Small business, organization, planning, marketing

Dom Teich, https://domteich.com/media-interviews
Fighter pilot, author, business owner, mindset

Jamarrion Tabor, info@mhousechildcare.com
Early childhood education, childcare coaching

Candace White, candace.white@startmail.com
Law, military justice, mental and physical health

Kevin Stokes, interviewkevin@bluehorizonnotes.com
Real estate notes, seller financing, creative terms

John Klesaris, meetjohn@aqwalker.com
Systemizing business for success, the military way

Mike Steadman, mike@weareironbound.com
Veteran, business, brand strategy, coach, author

Gary T. Dyer, freedomwithgary@gmail.com
Leadership, management, sales, and marketing

A SMALL REQUEST

Thank you for reading *I Love America*! I have a simple, quick request. Would you mind taking a minute or two and leaving an honest review for this book on Amazon? Reviews are the BEST way to help others make the decision to buy and support this book. Visit:

https://ILoveAmericaBooks.com/book1

If you have any questions or if you would just like to tell me what you think about *I Love America*, shoot an email to team@iloveamericabooks.com. We would love to hear from you!

Also, if you or anybody you know might be interested in purchasing bulk copies of this book, send an email to the address above and let us know. Thanks!

AN INVITATION TO BE A CONTRIBUTING AUTHOR IN A FUTURE EDITION!

If you would like to be considered for the opportunity of being a contributing author in a future edition of *I Love America*, please let us know!

We have plans for several themed editions of *I Love America*, each featuring 13 contributing authors sharing their stories, ideas, tips, and reader challenges for a stronger America.

Each edition of *I Love America* is "author-funded," meaning a portion of the expense of creating and publishing the book is shared by all the authors.

Fill out the Contributing Author Information Invitation by visiting:

ILoveAmericaBooks.com

Made in the USA
Las Vegas, NV
10 November 2022